T0132279

Into the Light;

Phoenix Rising

Memoir of a Medium's Journey

Louise Crandall

BALBOA.PRESS

A DIVISION OF HAY HOUSE

Balboa Press books may be ordered through booksellers or by contacting:

Balboa Press
A Division of Hay House
1663 Liberty Drive
Bloomington, IN 47403
www.balboapress.com
1 (877) 407-4847

Print information available on the last page.

ISBN: 978-1-9822-4472-9 (sc)
ISBN: 978-1-9822-4473-6 (e)

Balboa Press rev. date: 03/11/2020

CONTENTS

ACKNOWLEDGEMENTS

This book would not be possible without certain players in my life: my development circle of three years who supported each other in every undertaking. My close friends with whom I ran ideas through. I'd like to acknowledge and thank my mentor Mavis Pitilla and Jean Else. Their knowledge and inspiration kept me on my path. I'd also like to thank Chris Drew who was the final push to get me to put a pen to paper.

I also would like to thank those in my spirit tribe who have gently pushed me forward to learn and grow and serve and to accept beyond any doubt that life exists after this earthly journey.

Any inquiries should be directed to http://www.louisecrandall.com

1

The Beginning

My name is Louise and I was born prematurely on November 3, 1946. My middle-class parents were eager to receive their second child. My sister Linda was also born prematurely, one year before me. I guess we were both eager to start our journey! Astrologically, I'm a Scorpio sun with a Cancer moon –loaded with lots of water which symbolically translates to emotion. The independence and stubbornness of my Sun did not bode well for my parents and would rule my life for quite a while. Looking back, I certainly wasn't conscious of my early years as I was one huge emotional package, experiencing the ups and downs of my life as they happened. We lived in a small cape and Dad went to work every day, traveling a half hour or more each way, so when he got home, he needed to relax and unwind. He still had time for his girls though and we had a joyous time until we reached puberty and then things changed; but I get ahead of myself. Dad was never sad that he had all girls as he only knew boys growing up, but he was a little intimidated about the differences.

There were twin boys, Gary and Bobby who lived a couple houses down from us and Mom was friends with their mother, Mrs. Peterson. I thought the boys were the best thing since sliced bread because they shared the same sense of adventure that I did. They were lucky enough to have a yellow canary and a big cat. One day we decided to climb up to the kitchen sink and give the canary a bath in our cupped hands. The bird didn't appreciate it and the cat was sitting there waiting for a wet bird to fall into its outstretched paws. But Mrs. Peterson caught us and shooed us out.

We were close enough to kindergarten that we could all walk together because we were all the same age. One day we decided to skip kindergarten and go play at a nearby stream and just laugh and talk and skip stones. But of course, the teacher let Mom know and she and the teacher came looking for us. I rarely thought ahead about what would be the consequences of my actions. My fun was always spoiled. I wasn't allowed to nap in kindergarten either, as the teacher couldn't wake me up. Sleeping was a drug even back then. I could sleep for hours and I'm sure I was off somewhere in my dreams and fantasies.

There was a lovely older couple across the street from our house. Mr. Freetop used to grow the finest green beans, so tall that he had to use a ladder to pick them. Mrs. Freetop was interested in antique glassware like Mom and Dad, so they would often shop and compare their purchases. Grandma always knew where to find the bargains. They were Grandma and Grandpa to us because they seemed really old, and the closest we had at the time for a Grandmother and Grandfather. Our real grandfather and grandmother lived farther away and we didn't get to see them as much as we wanted. The Freetops had the neatest cuckoo clock on their front porch with the little people marching out on the hour. What fun! And Grandma always had a candy jar full of horehound drops, which is an acquired taste. The drops were in a cute antique candy jar that looked like a pineapple, which I now am fortunate to own. It is the only thing I have of theirs. When Mrs. Freetop was missing her husband, she knew he was over at our house watching baseball and having a beer with Mom. I think back then her favorite team was the Brooklyn Dodgers. Even later on in life, she could tell me her favorite stars, Pee wee Reese, Jackie Robinson, Duke Snider and Sandy Koufax. That is one love I inherited from her and later on in life she loved the Red Sox and especially Mookie Betts.

2

Middle Years

Eventually my parents bought a new house in the suburbs, a housing complex that used to be farmland, in fact part of it was still used as farmland and we used to go see the cows and the cow plops. It was on a corner lot and Dad had to mow the lawn every week and would be pretty angry when the neighborhood dogs would come and do their business where he had to mow. He thought he got even though when he bought manure and distributed it all over the lawn as fertilizer and would watch the dogs come over and roll in it before they went on their merry way home. He probably did get even with the dogs' parents who let them roam free! We would stay in that house for many years. All the surrounding families bought when Dad did and they all had children our age so we made lots of friends in the neighborhood. We wouldn't stop playing outside until it was dinnertime and Mom or Dad hollered at us to come in. Back then, bedtime was at 8:00PM sharp. I think the adults just wanted to get rid of us and have some peace and quiet.

One of the reasons we moved was to be closer to my grandfather and grandmother and, in addition, we could walk to the nearby new grammar school. Now we could see our real grandparents more often. To us, our home and property seemed adventurous with lots of rooms, a cellar, garage and tons of land. We would each have our own room which Dad and Grandad finished off, making the walls out of knotty pine. I used to like the smell of it. We did have a dark closet in the hallway which used to terrify me, though I'm not sure why. Maybe because it was dark and lots of clothes hung in there, and as Dad said, I had a vivid imagination. That would be a theme of his as I grew older, probably because of what came out of my mouth at times!

Holidays were always great celebrations. At Christmas, I remember our stockings filled to the brim and presents covering half of the room. We never lacked anything. Linda and I would try and stay awake to see Santa, but we never made it. There would always be homemade sugar cookies waiting there for him to have a little nourishment on his big night. Mom made them from scratch and, of course, left out a glass of Milk as well. We could not open any gifts until after breakfast, but we could come downstairs and get our stockings and go back upstairs. Mom and Dad were awake the whole time, but always pretended to be asleep. I know It was a joy for them also.

I remember when I was older, I wanted a two-wheel bike. Well, when I came downstairs, no bike was in sight. After everything was opened, Dad said, I think there is something for you in the basement. I went downstairs and there was a bike, albeit only half assembled. Still, I was overjoyed. I guess Dad hadn't had time to completely put it together. He was a little frustrated by the directions and had stayed up very late trying to get it done. He wanted to help me learn how to ride but I would have nothing of it. I would put the bike next to the back steps and hop on and keep pedaling by myself until I got it. It took several tries but I was stubborn and wanted to do it myself.

We always had family meals at Christmas, Thanksgiving, Easter, and on Sundays we had a family dinner after church. Linda and I learned to cook from observing Mom and carried a love for making meals throughout our adult life. Mom couldn't boil water when she met my Dad but she learned to cook from my grandfather. My biological grandmother died when Dad was about eight, so Grandaddy had to learn how to take care of his two boys by himself. He learned to cook, and obviously, he learned very well, although he had help along the way with relatives and probably other females he befriended. As a side note, after he passed, Linda and our cousin Jeff found a public record that stated a Charlotte was living with him after my biological grandmother had passed. This puzzled us because we knew that Charlotte was the name of my deceased grandmother's sister who was also dead. I guess he needed to account for the female living in the house when census takers came to call. He visited us one night in a mediumistic practice, and I asked him who she was. He chuckled that we knew about it, and said, "a man's got to do what a man has to do to raise two boys". Another side to my grandfather was revealed. He was thrilled to have female grandchildren he could dote on though.

At that point, I was probably around 8 and I seemed to still be living primarily by feelings and I was not cognizant of what I was saying at times. Apparently, I was so chatty, my dad always told me, "Children should be seen, and not heard." This hurt my feelings and stayed with me a good part of my life, even into adulthood. I wanted to talk about everything I saw and did and everything I was learning and also talk about some strange things to them that they didn't understand. I'm sure I questioned and talked about the "people" in my room at night. I never saw them, that I could remember, but I always heard them talking amongst themselves. This apparently was my first foray into the world of spirits. It didn't frighten me, in fact, I thought it was just a-matter-of- fact. I called them the gypsies and to this day have no reason why. One was a female voice and for some reason, I named her Charmaine. I used to get annoyed that they were chatting while I was trying to sleep, as sleep was always important to me! To this day, I have trouble falling asleep on Sunday nights, although now, there is a huge tribe of people with me. To my surprise, the name Charmaine would appear later on in life.

6

On the weekend I remember occasional trips to our nearby amusement park which sported a really tall wooden rollercoaster. I loved the speed and the height and took the wild trip over and over again until I was told "that is enough." The park was really cool, one of the oldest in the country, and is still a working amusement park, although I'm not sure if the rollercoaster is still working. Hopefully, it has been updated! It's wonderful to be young and throw yourself into something exciting, not worrying about speed and heights. I remember my first plane ride. I thought it was great when we took off and landed because that's when you could really "feel" the ride. That has changed. Now I'm a nervous flyer especially since I know most plane accidents happen when either landing or taking off. Isn't knowledge wonderful!

We also got to go to Dad's office picnics in the Summer which was always fun, except for the sunburns. I must have burned my nose 100 times when growing up; I guess because it stuck out more than the rest of my features. It took a while to get there and I got bored, usually kicking the seat in front of me which offended Dad, who hollered at me to stop. Occasionally his arm would come swinging from the front seat and crack me on the leg. I never thought that he was looking in the rearview mirror! I always had too much energy except when I was sleeping.

My respite came with my grandmother and grandfather. I loved them to death. There were no boundaries put on me, only love. My Grandad only had boys, so when little girls came into his life, he could shine. He used to tease us and joke with us. He did the same thing to his cats who to us were huge and you couldn't pet them as they didn't take well to his teasing either! We were easy prey to his jokes. He used to tweak my nose and I absolutely hated it, but that's why he did it. He would hand me a glass of buttermilk and ask me to try it, knowing I would be gagging in a minute. I was so easy.

My grandmother was a happy, loving lady. Even though we weren't hers biologically, she took us under her wing. We often had dinners together. She was the best pie maker although sometimes made errant decisions, like broiling the meringue on a lemon pie and burning it, (she always used Lard in her piecrust which made it really flaky and Linda would try it later on in life but it tasted just like Lard. Some things are meant to stay in your memory), or the pea soup would spray all over the ceiling from opening the pressure cooker too soon. We used to go for rides with her and she would check out the boys our age and honk at them if she thought we liked them, while we would slink down into the seat and hide, in case we knew them. Both Grandmommy and Granddaddy smoked like chimneys and every dress Grandma owned had cigarette burns in it. They were one of the joys of my life and Granddaddy stayed with me always.

It seemed like every Summer we took a trip with them. Money was tight, so Mom always packed breakfast and lunch for us as we tended to leave in the middle of the night. I sat in the back seat with my head on Grandmommy's lap and slept a good part of every trip. I thought the long drive was boring and also when Dad was driving, I could sleep. I never found another person I trusted driving while I slept. Dad used to take a route that had no facilities. We used to dash into the woods to relieve ourselves and arrive at the end of the route on fumes before we found a gas station. Dad had a habit of pushing the limits when it came to gas tanks. It was a game with him.

We used to visit a cousin of Grandad's. My sister got her middle name from our cousin's mother. At that point, some of Grandad's relatives were still living. We would stay in different cabins on the way. We thought most of them were scary places and sometimes stayed awake all night, waiting for the boogeyman to get us. Of course, Grandaddy made it worse, telling us ghost stories when Mom and Dad weren't around. I'm sure those shabby cabins have all disintegrated by now because it looked to me like they were halfway there already but they were inexpensive and relatively clean.

These were happy times, traveling with my grandparents, although my Dad would get exasperated with his Dad as Grandad had no patience. He would be getting out of the car before it came to a full stop. I think I inherited some of that impatience, although I spent a good part of my later life practicing patience. He still would remind me of that even after he was no longer in the earth plane. I'd hear from his spirit, especially when I was taking an important step.

Family was very important, also pets. We had a bird named Polly. A parakeet. She was the smartest bird I've ever seen and probably started my obsession with birds. When Dad would read the paper, she would sit at the top of it and peck at the paper as he turned it, hopping from one page to another. Sometimes when Mom would have a beer, she would sit on the edge of the glass and take a sip now and then. Polly had free range of the house when out of her cage. I remember they got her from a parakeet farm out in the country. We also had a cat named Tiger because he looked like a tiger. I was horribly allergic to cats and had to sleep with two pillows because of asthma. Back then, we didn't correlate asthma with allergies. That cat went everywhere. We would take a vacation to the beach and the cat would go with us, as would all the branches of our family. We would rent a cottage and they would come too, all close together, so we could get together on the beach and at night to play cards and drink. Mom would always bring a big pot of spaghetti sauce and others would bring bread and wine. It was a great time. Sometimes my Aunt would drink too much wine and get on the table and dance, which was hard for her because she had a lame leg but that never stopped her. Dad never drank or smoked but he did love being with his family. Playing cards was a big part of our early learning. The whole family played canasta and whenever grandparents were there, we all played. We were all competitive too. (To this day!) We would play partners and Dad, to his dismay, a lot of times got partnered with Grandmommy. She would go out without asking and leave him with a bunch of cards. Feisty lady, she probably did it on purpose because she knew he would get upset.

It was always funny to us. Mom loved gin rummy and Dad played hearts at work with his coworkers at lunch. He took cards seriously.

This was when I was entering middle school and when Dad decided he needed to teach us how to behave. I'm sure it was his way of protecting his girls but it had the opposite effect on me. He became really strict and it seemed to me, he didn't love me anymore. This pushed me more towards hating authority figures and wanting to do everything my own way. We couldn't talk at the dinner table. We had to eat everything put in front of us. We'd get that spiel, "If you lived during the depression, you would eat everything on your plate". I remember quietly keeping fat in the corner of my mouth and spitting it out when we were released from the dinner table. There were also times we'd get a crack on our knuckles with a fork or spoon if we spoke up. My little spirit was pushed lower and lower, until eventually it would disappear. One should never take away a child's sense of wonder and excitement in life. There are better ways to manage a curious child.

Mom wasn't as hard as Dad and she used to be the "go between" when we wanted something. She would carefully intervene with Dad. Having been a free spirit herself, I know she understood how hard it was for me, and tried to alleviate the pain of subordination. This would be the beginning of me striving for freedom and a relentless subconscious path of doing things my way took over, most of the time to my detriment. I'm sure at this point, my guardian angels and spirit tribe were gathering the forces for what they knew was coming.

This was around the time we first saw the movie, *Gone with the Wind*. I absolutely related to that movie. I loved the Scarlett O'Hara character and couldn't stand prissy Miss Melanie. I didn't understand why Scarlett always went after Ashleigh when Rhett Butler was the man of my dreams. Yes, I loved the bad-boy type and from that point on, was never interested in the "good" boys at school. It was always the hoods, with the ducktail haircuts, tight pants and pointed shoes. I was very immature and had no clue for a very long time about boys, birds and bees, and the repercussions of my choices.

I was always smart and loved English, grammar and spelling. I could spell with the best of them. The teachers always told my parents, "She's not applying herself; she can do much better". But I was bored. I didn't see how a lot of the school work would help me in my adult life. To this day, I still classify certain information I'd learned as trivia and had to decide whether to keep it in my brain bank or not. I was a true tomboy, and everyone called me "Wheezie." I loved to get out there with the boys and girls and play softball, ride my bike and never come in until dark or when we were called in to supper. In the winter we didn't have an ice-skating rink, but there was a swamp not far from our school which froze during the winter months and we would race around on our ice skates, jumping the stumps, having a grand time. I never would have been able to skate in a proper rink or in a straight line.

During middle school, around age 12 or 13, I felt more and more repressed in my spirit, though I never put a name to it. I became uninterested in anything at home and just wanted to get away from the anxiety I felt there. I used to watch the "hoods" smoking cigarettes before school, that is, if they actually showed up. I knew where they hung out at night and sometimes during the day. They knew me because I tried to connect with them and I'm sure I was an object of curiosity to them. One day I decided to leave home and never come back and ended up at the hangout store and they saw an opportunity for some free fun at my expense but I was completely unaware of their motivations and stayed with one of them. He had an apartment near the store. I can remember lying on the bed with him and knowing what he wanted, but I just ignored it. I was so innocent and luckily for me, he was not an abuser. I would look out the window and see the police and my parents driving by, looking for me. I felt happy but also worried at what I'd done. I eventually went home as there was no purpose to my running away, at least I didn't recognize it. Just exploration. Of course, I had to face my parents in a difficult scene, with a lot of tears from Mom and anger from Dad. My sister was noncommittal. She thought I had a screw loose and was disturbing her life. At this point in my journey, I was a rebellious adolescent and Mom and Dad were at a loss as to what to do with me. I had no use for school, especially when we kids knew one of our teachers drank when he had the chance, and ate sen sen candy to try and cover the smell on his breath. We never told our parents until much later in life, as they probably wouldn't have believed us. They asked me if I wanted to go to a private school; evidently they had been researching what to do with me. They wanted me to settle down and also wanted their life back in order. I agreed, as I'm sure I thought it was an opportunity for another adventure and a way out of the humdrum of my life.

3

The Dark Years

I 've been delaying writing this chapter. Now when I look back, I see that my guardians watched out for me and kept me from death. Literally. They, and I, had bigger plans, unbeknownst to me. It is still disturbing to my soul.

So, my parents packed me up and took me to a private school. I remember feeling they didn't love me or want me and it hurt deep down to my soul but I decided to block it out, curtain going down. That denial became a mantra in my thoughts going forward. I met a girl named Jill and we quickly became friends. She had the same attitude I did. Pretty, top heavy with dark hair, she was similar to me as I had long black hair, pretty and skinny. We made a good pair. As we went forward with classes in high school, we both decided it wasn't for us, especially when we heard that no-one had ever successfully run away from the school. Apparently, that was only a message not to try it, as we just walked away one night and hitched into the City and ended up at the bus station. Two small town pretty teenage girls, easy prey for those looking for easy prey! They found us immediately. We didn't know what to do once we got there, so two guys named Juan and Mario talked us up, bought us drinks and said they had a place to stay if we were looking. Mario was a dark haired relatively nice-looking guy in his late twenties and he took a liking to Jill. Juan, on the other hand, had short hair, tough with tattoos, a little scary, and he had his eye on me. I should have listened to that little voice of intuition saying *run*. The school reported us missing and my parents were told, and they tried to find us also but those were the days of no social media or internet so it was just word of mouth. They basically had to wait until we surfaced.

We went back to Mario and Juan's apartment, a two bedroom from what I can recall. We were paired up and virginity quickly flew out the window and not in a nice way. It began nicely enough but Juan was definitely showing me I was his and would do whatever he wanted me to do. Both guys smoked pot and I remember trying it once but didn't like it as it was too strong and I felt I lost control of my mind. Mario would be happy when he smoked but when Juan smoked or drank, he was mean. I can only say that back in that time, I hardened myself and my protective curtain came down. I still went about like a puppet but had to stuff my feelings or I would go mad. It was a dumpy apartment and there was never any money. We ate a lot of beans and rice and tortillas which was very good, made the proper way. To this day, when I go to a restaurant, I judge their authenticity by the way beans taste.

Because of the barrier I put between myself and the world, it's hard for me to recall, but I know Juan had a side business, a steady business of selling heroin. He was partners with an older guy named Ray and his live-in black wife named Cookie. I didn't see them much. Juan would take me to the bars and he would drink and have fun with all his friends and then would grab me and take me into the alley and start punching me in the head if he felt like it. Just because he could. I still remember how a fist to the head feels, like you've slammed into a brick wall! It was the only thing he knew, with his crude lifestyle, how to control what he thought was his. I wonder to this day why I'm not a vegetable. One day, when he ordered me into the alley, I wouldn't go. He came back in and said, "you know if you came with me, I would have hit you." Duh! There must have been an angel intervention.

We never had any money and it was winter. I had no coat, so one day we walked past this office and he saw a coat hanging on a rack by the door and slipped in and got me a coat to wear. He had to protect his investment. It was then that I knew what he had in mind for me. He rented a cheap hotel room and became a pimp. He put me in the hotel room and told me to collect the money before I let them touch me and he would pimp on the corner and send men up for sex. I remember just lying there like a doll, feeling demeaned and disgusted while strange men did whatever they wanted. I was thankful that I had put up that curtain around my sensitive nature and any feelings. Later in life, I called it my shelter from the storm. I would use that throughout my life when I had to make a hard decision. I would find out later on, that Mom had the same capacity! I felt I had no choice in my life. I was afraid of Juan and he always said if I left him, he would hunt me down and kill me. To this day, I understand how abused women stay with their abuser through fear, caught in the loop of abuse and fear without an iota of self-worth, feeling like there is no one to help them. But there is . . .

I remember once the police picked me up thinking we had drugs. That was another humiliation, the female cop searching every crevice looking for drugs. That was an opportunity for me to get help but I never realized it since I was so ensconced in the horror of my life. They never pressed charges as they never found anything and life continued on. Partner Ray decided to take a trip as he had business elsewhere. He took me in the car and Juan was going to join us. Mario and Jill stayed since Mario had a regular job. They did find a different place to live. While on our car trip, the police raided our apartment and took the heroin and Juan. I wonder now if Ray knew this was going to happen and got me out of there, or if it was angel intervention again that put that idea in Ray's head. Juan was not emotionally stable and Ray was much different as he ran a business and did not want to make waves at all. That would be the end of my relationship with them because when we arrived, I contacted my Uncle who had a house in the suburbs and he met me and took me to his house. My cousin was a little younger than me and I can remember being under her bed where she kept all of the sweets that her Mom wouldn't allow her to have. After I took a complete bath and put on new clothes, I ate and laughed with her. My parents had been frantically searching for me and I guess things at home for my sister were not good. I had been gone for at least one and a half years. A lot of her anxiety and anger and emotional trauma, of course, rightfully so, she blamed on me. Mom was a very emotional person anyway and she was pushed to her limits not knowing where I was. My uncle George, a kind, generous, non-judgmental man, talked to me frankly to see if I wanted to go home and I agreed. So back home I went.

Mom and Dad were grateful I was home. My sister was glad life might go back to normal for her without the stress from our parents affecting her life. She would never divulge her feelings. I guess she had a sort of hurt barrier too, as she maintained it throughout life. I never knew what she was thinking unless she was spitting mad. She was in high school and enjoying her time there. She had a new friend who moved in a street over from us and they spent a lot of time together. But for me, things hadn't changed. I was still in limbo it seemed. I couldn't stand the thought of going back to public school at home, wondering what people would think happened to me. I remember thinking they probably thought I got pregnant and went away to have the child. Far from the truth! Back then I cared what people thought of me. I was still so sensitive, and even more-so after my experiences. Luckily Juan didn't know where I came from or lived, as I was sure he would have made his threat to kill me a reality. I did miss my freedom though. One day, I was arguing with my mother about how no-one understood me and how I felt like I was in chains, doing what everyone else wanted me to do. She was quite upset about it. When my father came home, he came upstairs to my room with a belt in his hands and said "this is going to hurt me more than it hurts you" and he went on to hitting me on the legs with the belt and telling me what damage I did to my mother when I was gone, that she had a nervous breakdown, and he would not permit me to do that again. It may have hurt him to do that, but believe me, it hurt me too and I will never forget it. No child deserves to be beaten, even mildly so as my father did. There is always a way to get through the trying times without it. I'm sure people thought I was a meanspirited child, only thinking of myself, but that was not quite accurate. I was thinking of myself in the context of wanting to feel loved and not wanting restrictions on my spirit, although I didn't realize what I did or didn't want at the time.

One day while Dad and Mom were working and my sister was at school, I called a cab and got out of Dodge, once again. I took a bus to the city and found a job in a local corner restaurant doing waitress work, even though I had no experience. It wasn't the type of restaurant where experience mattered, the management just needed a body. I got a room in a hotel. I had a fake license that said I was eighteen when I was actually sixteen.

4

The Gray Years

It didn't take me long to realize I couldn't pay bills working in the sleazy restaurant, so one day I was walking by a dance hall that was looking for dancers. I went upstairs and filled out an application. No real experience was needed there either but I was just what they were looking for, as long as I had identification saying I was over age 18. I was a clean-cut kid who looked fabulous in a tight little dress. I didn't wear a lot of makeup as I didn't need to. The owner/manager, Tony, took me under his wing, so to speak. He had beautiful blue eyes and dressed to the nines and thought he was Frank Sinatra. He even sang sometimes at the club. He was what I believed to be a typical gangster and had all the connections to prove it. He was married with a little boy but really liked me and decided I wasn't going to get into the general milieu of the dance hall. Supposedly that's all it was. Men would come and buy tickets to dance with the women of their choice, and of course, the women would hang over the bars and try to entice them. Not me. But there were a couple that weren't looking for sex, just a dance with a pretty girl. But I'm getting ahead of myself. Tony and I became a quiet item. He got me a studio apartment in between a fire station and police station, so I felt pretty secure there. I weighed 110 and walked everywhere and got to know about life in the city. I loved the Chock

Full of Nuts coffee stands on the corners, and got my coffee there every morning with real cream and sugar. To this day, I don't leave the house without my coffee.

I thought I loved Tony. Although he was old enough to be my father, he was kind and generous and took care of me. He kept me away from the perverts at work and the only thing he expected was for me to be true to him. I had no problem with that. He smelled so good. He wore an aftershave that was a combination of musk and vanilla. I still can't remember what the name of it was, but I always remembered the smell. I tried not to think about the wife and child at home. It was the old story of how she didn't understand him, yada, yada, yada. Once again, I didn't really have my freedom and was still subservient to someone, but in a different way, despite the fact that I never realized that. In fact, I never really understood until late in my life that like many women, I had fallen into a psychological syndrome. I did whatever Tony wanted me to do, but it was a loving relationship as he was kind, caring and considerate of me and my feelings.

A few months into the relationship, I found myself pregnant. I was out of my mind, wondering what to do. Of course, Tony had a plan. Abortion was illegal back then. But he had a friend, a woman friend who apparently was a fixer for him. All I wanted was for the problem to go away. I didn't think of the consequences. His fixer knew a doctor who would perform the abortion, so that's what happened. I went to the fixer's apartment, and on her kitchen table, had the abortion. Subservient! Humiliated! Sad. Later in life, I knew abortion was something I did not agree with, but I will fight for the rights of women to make their own choice. I made a wrong choice, and had to live with it. Later on, I was told I had so much scar tissue that I could never conceive. I stayed with the fixer a couple of days to be sure I was all right. Physically I was, but mentally and emotionally, I was not so good. Of course, these people had to be paid, so Tony knew a Shylock (that's what they were called in those days!) and he had to be paid back, with exorbitant interest, a reminder of what I'd done.

Tony drove a cab as his Father held a tight rein on finances. One day I was waiting for him and he showed up really late. He told me he hit a child with his cab, not seriously, but he was devastated and cried when he told me. He bought him toys and went to see him in the hospital. The parents were ever so kind and knew he had darted out with nowhere for the cab to go, but that is not something you forget if you have a heart and a conscience.

Life continued for us. I became a little more independent since Tony had to be with his family. There was a nice business man who came into the dance hall who was very proper and just wanted company. He asked me if I would accompany him to a play and I said yes. So off we went. I met him at the theatre and he was pleased to see me. He gave me a gold bracelet as a gift. I'm sure if I offered more to him, he would take it, but he seemed satisfied with just my company. I felt certain other dancers did more than just accompany men, although I had no clear proof of that. They all wanted to dance with a skinny little millionaire who was well known in the dance club but he only had a certain "type" that he was attracted to, and I happened to be the type. He seemed a little shady to me but he always acted like a gentleman talking to me about his life. He asked me to come up to his penthouse one time just for a drink. I said yes, just because I wanted to see a penthouse. When I arrived, the doorman brought me up and I met John there. He showed me around and started talking about a new pharmaceutical drug he was working on and wanted to know if I would try one. He said there were no side effects but they couldn't do human trials yet, so naive idiot I was, I tried it. It really had no effect on me. He was into health and used to do a sauna and then lay out in the snow. Really a "funny" man. Everyone has their little hidden fantasies, I guess. Apparently, Tony was looking for me when I was gone and when I did tell him about my little adventure, he was furious and scared for my welfare and I'm sure he was a little disconcerted as well that I stepped over the boundaries he set forth in our relationship. But he got over it.

I was feeling a little homesick, so I called my grandmother and told her where I was. She was so happy to hear from me and said she would call Mom and Dad. After a while, I heard from Mom and she wanted to visit and bring my Aunt and grandmother with her so we planned a date and time. They came by train and took a cab to my apartment. I showed them around and had lunch for them. My Aunt was one of my favorites. She never pressured me, just loved me and made the best macaroni and cheese! When they left, she accidentally took my purse with her, thinking it was my mother's. Although now I wonder if there was a scheme in place. They realized it later and sent it back in the mail. After that, my Mom and Dad would come visit. Right across the street was a Greek restaurant and Dad absolutely loved going there for the desserts, especially the custard ones. That love for pastries I inherited from him! I guess they were reconciled to the fact that I was living in the city and none the worse for wear. But they did say to come back home, any time I wanted.

Day in, day out, my routine was stable for quite a while. I was used to working the graveyard shift and enjoying my days off. However, then life turned around when someone from the club told me Tony's wife was pregnant. I was devastated, hurt, betrayed, and angry. He tried to explain it away, saying it was nothing, he just had to keep up the facade of a happy home. I made my plan to leave and go back home and he had no knowledge of those plans and wouldn't find me. I took my belongings and took a bus back home and Mom picked me up. I was older now, and a little more mature. I resolved to make things work this time. I found out a few months later that Tony contacted my grandmother, not sure how he got her name or number, and she actually thought he was cool. I would also find out later, that he was sending her gifts like candy and scotch. She told me how sorry and upset he was and asked if I would, at least, see him. I did finally say yes. He was taking flying lessons and flew down to the local airport where I met him and he took me for a ride in his little plane. It was amazing but I was very nervous. It didn't change anything though. I told him never to contact me or my family again. He made his bed, he needed to sleep in it. And that was it. Curtain down.

5

Young Adult Years

I got a job at a clock factory that was converted to a bomb-making business. It was definitely the most boring job I ever had but I was also going to classes to get my GED while living at home. I used to sit on an assembly line and set the timing device on the heads of the bombs. I would fall asleep with the monotony of it all and I worried about the job I was doing. What if it didn't go off when it was supposed to and injured one of ours! It was around this time that my Dad got a call from my grandmother. Granddaddy had gotten up to feed the cats, made himself breakfast and went back to bed and died. He apparently had a heart attack. This was my first experience of someone I loved dying and I was devastated. My uncle George and his family arrived and there was the usual big funeral. We rode in a limousine to the cemetery and I was crying the whole time, wondering why my sister and cousins weren't as upset as I was. They just processed things differently and didn't get to see each other much, so while they were catching up, I was miserable.

Not long afterward, something happened that opened my eyes that made me think maybe death wasn't final. I came home from work exhausted and lay down on the couch to take a nap. All of a sudden, I awoke with a start as words were coming out of my mouth. "Hmm, my heart stopped." I knew it was my dear Grandfather telling me he was okay. His passing was just that, a passing. I wondered how he had so clearly communicated his thoughts as he passed. I knew he came to me because of our loving connection. Once my journey progressed, he would be more vocal. I never mentioned this to anyone until later on in my life, unless I mentioned it to Linda. I can't really remember. I'm an analyzer and analyze things to death, so a lot of what I saw and heard, I kept to myself until I thought it was the right time.

I passed my GED, received my diploma and registered for a one-year course in medical assistance at a local college. I found I was really interested in the medical field. Sequences are all a blur to me, but I went to work with Dad as a clerk in his office. We would have apple pie for breakfast and head out together. I guess he'd forgiven me for being so rebellious but it would be a long time before I realized what the effects of his comments, rules and regulations had on my life. Linda and I mended our relationship also, but I'm sure she was wary of what I would do next. She had gone to school for hairdressing and found a job in a local shop in our town. Back then, there was no creative license, all women wanted was to have their hair washed and set and blown dry. She did have fun in school and we tried every hair color and cut. It was a blast, and that probably is the reason, even today, why I'm never satisfied for long with my hair style or color. Also, back then I had a white streak in the front of my hair which was very peculiar and we didn't know what to do with it!

It was in the Summer when Mom got a call that her brother died. Dad came home from work. My uncle Ed was very close to Mom, in fact she lived with him when her father died, and he was a real father to her. I remember her shut up in her bedroom all day, just sobbing. We all loved our uncle. When we were little and visited him, he would sit us on his sight-seeing bus in the front with him and we got to see everything there was to see in Washington. He was a kind, loving, quiet man. I recall my Aunt Emily making sticky buns for us in the morning. My childhood was full of great memories along with the not so great ones. Mom was never the same. To her, his death was like losing a father, twice.

Linda and I had a friend named Bridget and we all talked about getting our own apartment. We were all working, and I was working plus going to school. I borrowed Mom's car to get back and forth to school. We found a three-bedroom apartment about 5 miles from where we lived. It was our first taste of freedom, so to speak. We had second hand furniture and took our beds from home. We had no pictures to put on the wall so we took pictures of ourselves and had them blown up to poster size and put them on the wall. We had our hair done, makeup on, and wore halter tops and tight pants. We thought we looked great! We painted bricks red and made a bookcase. It was fun. The apartment to the right of us belonged to a lady from England named Polly who moved in with her husband and kids. She was so damn homesick; she became an easy friend. We also loved her accent, the way she talked, even though half the time we didn't know what she was saying. Her husband worked and the kids were in school, so she was lonesome. Aside from the odd book we read, she gave us our first taste of psychic phenomenon and spiritualism. We used to sit at her kitchen table with a hand-made Ouija board and it worked amazingly well. Back then we tried all kinds of communication with the other world and I was a little scared, but always called in my protector who was a cowboy named Sam. I would always see his hat and I knew he was there. Nowadays, I don't believe we need protection from anything evil in spirit. On earth is a different story.

She would help me with my homework for medical terminology. She used to act out the words and believe me, I never forgot them! For instance, rhinorrhea, she'd act like her nose was running and used her finger to come straight across and wipe it off! I loved her.

There was also an apartment of boys who moved in upstairs and to the left of us. Of course, we thought they were fun. They were going to the local college and they had good parties and played the guitar and sang. This was the era of the 60's, hippies, free love, free pot and abandonment. Harry was captivated by his gas passing. He was funny and innocent, and our friend Bridget had the same sense of humor and got along well. Allen and my sister started seeing each other. He was a Brainiac but when he had too much to drink, he would play Janis Joplin tunes on his guitar. We loved her wildness and her music. We actually got to see Janis at the local Civic Center when she was with Big Brother and the Holding Company. Music had always been a big part of my life. We grew up listening to big bands, Frank Sinatra, and others from my parents' era but we loved the new soul music and popular music of our time. When James Brown came on the scene, we were enthralled with his antics and swinging around his cape. Too funny. Allen also loved and introduced us to Bob Dylan. This is where my sister and I differ. She knew what she wanted in life and went after it. I drifted around like a tumbleweed looking for what I thought was love. She decided she didn't like hairdressing and set her eyes on someone who would earn a living so she didn't have to ever work again. And that someone was Allen. He would graduate and become a teacher. But first, he was going to get drafted, so he enlisted in the air force. All of our lives had changed and our relationship with our friend Bridget fizzled so Linda and I moved back home, so did Bridget.

Our English friend Polly moved into another apartment on the other side of town. But we kept in touch. Allen and Linda became engaged. Of course, we had to meet his parents and there was an engagement party at our house to which they drove down to. It was a little difficult for them as they were country folk who rarely left the town they were brought up in, which happened also to be Allen's home town. When they drove down, they saw the first sign for our town and got off, and of course, it wasn't the right exit. There were no cell phones in those days, so they had to get help from someone to get back onto the highway and continue on their way. They were not brainiacs like Allen, just simple folk who brought their family up in a small town with nothing in it. Different folks. Not that we were well traveled but we were used to going here and there on vacation. Allen took off for basic training and was eventually stationed out west, which felt way across the world from us. Linda and I bought a car together. A Buick Regal Ragtop. It was a great car. She missed Allen so much, they made plans to get married in Texas.

My parents were unhappy that they chose to get married by a justice of the peace, without them there. This was another thing they had to get over. Linda and I made plans to drive her out and I would fly back. Dad went to AAA and got a map and mapped out our route. He gave us money and told us when we stopped for the night to call collect and then he would check on his map to see where we were. That way we would check in and he would not accept the charges, but he couldn't help himself. He always accepted the call and was anxious to hear where we were. I was a good driver even back then and I enjoyed it. Linda, on the other hand, tried to do her part but when I saw the tears forming in her eyes, I would take over the wheel and she was grateful. Even later in life, I continued to do the driving and she was content to direct and play navigator.

We arrived and Allen took us to his apartment. The wedding was set for the next day with a couple of his friends as witnesses. We took a lot of pictures for our parents and I left them there with the car to start their new lives together and flew home. I thought it would be pretty boring there because it was the Bible belt and no hard liquor was sold for miles. They had no choice but to get to know each other. Yikes!

I came back home, finished school, and did very well because I resonated with the medical subject and one particular teacher, Mrs. Weeks. I still worked with Dad and looked for a job in my new field. That summer we occasionally went to family picnics, usually held at my Aunt Noreen's house. She was the favorite Aunt who visited me in New York. She shared a driveway with her niece and her mother, my great Aunt Dora. She was really old and a true character. In fact, all my relatives were characters. I remember Aunt Dora hanging tea bags on the clothes line to dry and be reused. She had grey hair and always wore dresses and when she just smelled wine or booze, she could dance with the best of them. Anyway, the family picnics were always held there because they had an acre of land in the back of the two houses and loads of people could come and they did from far and wide. Aunts, uncles and cousins I never saw too much and didn't remember. That is where I met my future husband David.

David was about four years older than me and a third or fourth cousin. He had a sporty car, a Charger I believe. I thought he was fun and cool. At first, the parents didn't think it was proper for us to date since we were cousins, but our relatedness was so far removed, they acquiesced. I loved that he was a happy person and acted like a kid, even though he was older. We got along well and he asked me to marry him. I loved his Mom and Dad. His mom was Dad's third cousin. We had a lovely engagement party and the one thing I recall is all the Grandmothers lined up on one side. His grandmother, mine, Grandma Freetop, and Great Aunt Dora. I still hold that picture in my brain. Great women. You could see their life experience and the great knowledge they held when you looked into their eyes.

We were married in the chapel of our Congregational church by my Uncle George, Dad's brother. We had a lot of preachers and ministers in our ancestry and George followed suit. Since they didn't live near us, we rarely got to hear him preach but I heard he was pretty interesting. Dad walked me down the aisle and we had a reception at the house afterwards.

David and I took off in his car up North for a honeymoon and did a lot of antiquing on the way. Those where the times when you could go to a barn and find good furniture. Most of our furniture was accumulated that way. We would take it home and refinish it. We both loved antiques. We got an apartment and I got a job in a local hospital. David didn't really have a higher education so he never held a steady job when we were together. I always had a continuous job as a radiology transcriber, which was not what I went to school for, but having the medical terminology certainly helped! We lived close to his parents and not far from work. I still kept in touch with Polly and we saw each other regularly because she bought a house not far from where we were living. David retained his childlike happy personality which grated on me eventually, because I didn't feel he was responsible. His grandfather was part Native American and he had an Indian guide, Chief, who showed up in his life when there was a need. That was the story anyway, since his grandad wasn't with us any longer. And since we were all interested in "the occult," as it was called then, we started to have seances. At first, we had them in Polly's cellar. We'd all sit around in the dark with our hands on a card table. It was pretty spooky for me. One time, I saw a child coming down the stairs and she came around to stand in back of my chair. Polly was sitting next to me. I thought it was my imagination. But later on, privately, Polly said to me, there is a girl that came down the stairs, and stood in back of you, is she yours? I remembered then the kitchen table abortion. I believe she was brought up in spirit with family and I once again felt sad and guilty. I was amazed Polly saw her too and saw her come around to stand behind me. We continued having seances with different friends and family joining us. When Allen got sent overseas, Linda came back home and she joined in. Dad thought it was hogwash but once in a while Mom would sit with us. I did not remember this until I found a picture of the little table up in the air and Mom's face in shock! We used to have the table dance all over the room so we had to throw our chairs back and walk with it. At first, I was always looking under the table to see if someone was manipulating things, but there never was anyone. It was spirit energy moving the table. We didn't know enough to ask questions at that time. We didn't know that spirits could communicate by answering our questions with the movement of the table. We never knew who was the mastermind behind it all, whether it be spirit or one of us being a physical medium.

David's grandmother died and she lived in a house three doors down from his Mom and Dad so we were able to buy it. David was looking for a full-time job to help support things. We set to refurbishing the house as it was very old and needed a lot of work. His Mom and Dad helped. It was a huge job. In the meantime, on weekends, we would visit Polly and Ben, her husband, and go to the small ranch in the area and go horseback riding. It was fun, although at first, I was so sore, I would come home and just sit in the shower. I always rode a horse named Sam whose only idea of fun was to knock me off from low hanging branches and head back to the barn. It seems the name Sam was prevalent in my life! We eventually purchased Sam and Chief, whom David rode. We boarded them for a while at the ranch because it was convenient and we knew the trails and could ride often. Eventually, Polly and Ben kept theirs at their house because they had a barn in the back and we boarded ours where they had a big field to run through and a beautiful area with lots of trails. Of course, we had to buy a horse trailer too. I still remember the great softness of a horse's nose. I cherish that memory.

David finally got a job driving a delivery truck, a steady, good paying job. He drove around all day and loved it. I thought, finally, he has a good, steady, job. One day over a year later, he told me he'd been fired. I couldn't believe it. I knew he was a good worker and enjoyed it. He finally told me there were workers that were stealing and he knew it and never said anything, so he got canned with the rest of them. That's when I had had enough. He never held down a job or helped support us. I felt like I was doing it all. I went over to his mother's house to explain my point of view, but she was crushed and blamed me for the marriage collapsing. I didn't care. I was out of there. Curtain down! Mom and Dad had moved to a smaller house with a barn so they could have an antique shop. I remember going over there for someone's birthday and just sat out front by myself, I was so miserable and felt like a failure. Dad came out and gave me a hug and asked me what was wrong, and told me everything was going to be all right. I remember thinking, My God, he does love me. It was the first time he let his guard down with me. I would remember that moment forever, that's how starved I was for his acceptance and love. It brought tears to my eyes. He would never know until he passed beyond the veil, what effect he had on my life and all that I had to unlearn. When he came through in spirit though, he recalled that conversation with me and apologized for it being so long in coming.

David and I divorced. It was not easy or nice. I just wanted out. I resolved to never go through that again.

Allen was stationed overseas and Linda decided to join him there. She got her passport and was ready to go. Allen was going to meet her plane. It was about an 18 hour trip. He kept meeting a plane and she never got off. She was so tired that she fell asleep on the plane and someone stole her passport. When she went to get off, she looked for it and it was gone. Here she was in a strange country with no identification. She was crying and a serviceman took pity on her. He gave her money and took her to the US embassy where she got a new passport. Then she got another flight. I could never imagine how horrible it was for her. I felt so empathic. It was like it happened to me and I could feel her pain and how frightened she was. That was when I became protective of her, even though she was older than I. Dad was so relieved, he got the name of the man who helped her, and reimbursed him for the money he spent as well as thanking him profusely for helping his daughter. I didn't hear too much from her while she was there. I guess it was kind of lonesome when Allen went on flights for weeks at a time, but she had friends and a dog that kept her company.

I got an apartment and continued working. I loved the doctors in our department but Fran, the woman who was the head honcho in our department, was demanding and very particular. It was very difficult working for her and my new coworker Mary was even more afraid of her. Mary and I became friends as she was single also. We used to take off at 8:00 at night and drive to a bar 30 minutes away and hang out there drinking and dancing all night and then go to work the next day. Those were the days I could stay awake! We met a couple of prison guards and carried on with them for quite a while until Mary found that hers was married! She was so devastated. Charlie wasn't. He had a motorcycle and we would ride sometimes. I can't remember what happened to him but he disappeared also. He was a free-spirited Aquarius. I had been studying astrology for a few years, mostly with good books that described the sun signs and rising signs and I had all the books to draw up my own charts as this was before there were computers that could do all the calculations for you. I have maintained that love of astrology, though I never fully learned about it professionally. I'm an observer of people and I began to intuitively see the similarities in the signs.

I kept up my friendship with Polly. She was well accustomed by now to living in America and was enjoying all that she never had in England. She was working, and we bowled together in a mixed league. She loved to fish in the stream behind her house. I hated anything to do with worms and couldn't stand bugs, so I did not join her, but we would just sit together for hours, drink tea and talk. She would talk about Ben because Polly liked people and socializing, having company and going out with a friend or group and Ben mostly liked to stay home. He did like me though. He was another water sign, a Cancer, so we had similar feelings, I guess. One night I had a few too many drinks, Manhattans which I'd never tried before, and I took Ben aside and told him all that was wrong with his marriage and what he could do to improve it. It's the first and last time I ever drank so much that I didn't know what I was saying. He was still friendly with me after that, so it couldn't have been too bad and Polly laughed about it. Me, the relationship expert giving advice!

6

Jobs and Changes

Linda came back because Allen would come home soon and she was pregnant! Everyone was so excited. She was big as a house and Allen would not make it home for the birth. We had a baby shower for her with the relatives closest to us and funnily enough, Fran, my supervisor from work, wanted to be included, so she came and brought a beautiful blanket. Fran was the one I talked about who was not easy to work with; was demanding and unfaltering in the way she saw things. I saw a different side of her and that should have been a lesson to me to look beyond the outer façade of people.

Linda's son was born in the hospital I was working at, with Mom by her side and me in the waiting room. She didn't want me to see, as she thought the pain involved would keep me from ever having children . . . She was protective of me too. *Funny that!* Her son was born and was the most beautiful baby we ever saw, a true Gerber baby, perfect in every way. Allen came home soon after, and they got an apartment a few hours from us so Allen could continue his education and go for a Master's degree. We were sad to see them leave us. Linda had her wish; she would stay home taking care of the house and her son and not having to work outside of home and she loved Allen. She was very good at making ends meet, very creative, and made a comfortable home with what she had.

I would visit Mom and Dad often, usually at dinner time so I could have a good cooked meal. Dad and I used to talk, and eventually our topics got around to my belief in life after death. He never believed it he said. For some reason though, he said if we have a "seance" again, he would join us. I think someone put a little bee in his bonnet. The next time we met, he joined us. We all sat around the table in a darkened room. It was never completely dark. We always just encouraged the spirits to show up. Eventually the table would start moving slightly from side to side; I could see Dad looking under the table. Eventually it would start rocking and making a loud noise while doing it, like it was going to split apart. When this started, we had to throw back our chairs and keep our fingers, or finger, lightly on the table and just go with it! Dad was amazed to say the least.

It was shortly after that, that Dad started to complain about headaches. Nothing could relieve them and Dad was not someone to complain. In time, He had a CAT scan and his doctors found a tumor in his brain. We contacted a neurosurgeon and he said the only thing they could do was operate, but that it would not cure the glioblastoma. (I would learn to hate that word.) He was scheduled for surgery and I remember the doctor telling me to wait to see him until the next day because brain surgery back then was very damaging to the brain and I didn't want to see him in recovery. Well, I didn't listen. Since I worked in the hospital, I had access to the recovery room.

That was when I realized our bodies are just machines, like a car to travel around in while we're here. I saw a vegetable in that bed and won't soon forget it; the surgeon was right. Dad stayed in the hospital for a week or so. He was in a room with a much younger man, with the same surgery. I felt bad for them both. Dad didn't really know anyone since the part of the brain affected was the communication part. But I remember walking in his room to make sure he got fed, and he actually looked at me and said "Hi Sweetie". My heart leaped.

It was just a fluke. Now, though, I think it was his Spirit making it through to communicate and acknowledge my presence. Through this whole period following the operation, he never complained of any pain, although the surgeon later told us he had to have pain. We knew he never wanted to be a burden. My sister came back to be with us during this hard time in our lives.

When Dad came home, Mom would help him with daily activities but he really couldn't speak too many sentences. For some reason, he was captivated by candles and the flickering flame. I wondered what he was thinking. Maybe "his" spark of light. I came over as much as I could to give her a break and just be with my family. Mom was a wreck at this time, and rightly so. I remember she went to the store and had to take Dad, because she couldn't leave him at home alone. She was in such a hurry to get back to the car, that she tripped and fell forward on her face. She was a bloody mess, but kept on going, simply came home and bandaged herself up. Dad was upset but didn't know what to do. I was visiting them one night and walked by his bedroom and heard him saying, "But what's she going to do with this house"? I knew he was getting his affairs in order and his time was getting close. I felt intuitively that he was speaking with his father and was trying to reconcile what Mom would do when he was gone. I mentioned to Mom what I heard him saying and she said that he was always talking to someone. I felt that his loved ones across the veil were preparing him to be with them once again. We never leave this world alone, no matter who you are or what you've done in this life. The pain and suffering at the end is erased from your memory.

He really got a charge out of his grandson Jim. Jim was a rambunctious child and it was hard to contain him, but he would sit on Dad's lap and be calm and serene. They both needed that time together. Dad got worse so back into the hospital he went. Most of his relatives came to see him, except his sister-in-law who said "Oh, I want to remember him the way he was". I never forgot that. To me it showed no respect for the ones he would leave behind. Sure, it's hard, but it's the last time in this world you can let your loved one know how you feel or say goodbye. Dad ended up catching pneumonia in the hospital, which is not unusual. I recall his surgeon stopping into my department to talk to me, telling me, (or asking me), we can either treat the pneumonia and prolong the life he has, or let him naturally go in comfort. I brought that information home to Mom and Linda and we decided not to treat the pneumonia.

When my sister's son Jim turned 2, Dad passed. It was a windy March day and I'm sure his spirit soared to meet those who had gone before him. He was only 56. I always think of him around Jim's birthday and when the March winds blow up a storm. It was a horrible time for all of us. Even though we believed he was going onward to resume a perfectly healthy life in another dimension, we missed his every day presence. He was buried in a plot in Waterbury with his Dad, his stepmother, and with room for his brother and his wife and for Mom as they were, or will be cremated. Lots of friends and family attended the memorial service including folks from work who were so supportive of Mom. He had worked there for many years and they loved him too. I was so grateful and glad that we had mended our relationship, and had a little time with each other in the end. I was also happy I worked in the hospital that took care of him so I could keep tabs on things.

The house was way too big for Mom to take care of, even with my help. They had a Christmas tree farm in the back and also the antique shop to the right of the driveway and were on a huge hill. We did have some good memories of all that took place in that home. When they first moved into the house, all of a sudden, in December, Dad looked out the kitchen window and saw people in the back where the trees were. He went out and asked what they were doing, and they said tagging their tree! Mom and Dad didn't even know the land with Christmas trees was part of the deal. They sold trees that year but stopped after that. They preferred the antique business which was fun for them. We all piled in the VW van and took off for a huge antiques show. This was back when it first started. We slept in the van and set up at night. That's when all the business took place. All the dealers walked around with their flashlights buying what they were interested in. It was a new experience for us but really fun. We came back with less than we took. They did a few shows here and there and really enjoyed looking up their prizes in antique books. It was a good business back then. Dad's brother moved closer, as he was a minister at a church not far from us. He enjoyed sometimes attending the shows with us too. As it turned out, he was quite the wheeler and dealer for a minister! We got a charge out of him. His daughter Cam was in college and rescued a dog that had been tied outside and was very fearful of being alone. Cam snuck her into her dorm room but eventually she got caught and her Dad couldn't take her because he already had a dog and didn't want another, so Mom and Dad took Goldie. She was the sweetest golden, but you couldn't leave her alone, so they took her everywhere.

Eventually, Mom sold the house and the antique shop. She kept some glassware that she liked and bought a house not far away. It was smaller, with not much of a yard though she had great neighbors who watched over her. Mom was pretty independent and knew how to take care of herself. Here she was at 56, buying a house on her own and taking off in her car to go see Linda and also driving down south to see her sister-in-law and her family as well as to see her sister. There was no stopping her. I wonder if she felt finally free to be herself and see her family more.

I was still working, and dating, but nothing serious. I would go bowling with friends, Polly, Connie and Nate. Occasionally, I bowled with Phil. It seemed I always had to have a man in my life. Being alone was not an option for me. Being picky was not an option either, since I never learned to love myself and there was that pattern of abuse that was ingrained in me from my earlier experiences in the city.

Mom decided she wanted to be closer to her grandson so she sold her house and bought a two family, two streets over from Linda. She already had a nice couple that was renting upstairs, so she was happy to be in a huge Victorian house with plenty of room downstairs for her and Goldie. If she needed work done, Allen was glad to help out. He wasn't very handy but he learned quickly how to do things. Linda always wanted painting done and sprucing things up and wasn't about to pay anyone to do it. They had bought a two family and the person upstairs moved out so they asked me if I wanted the apartment and I was glad to move to be near Mom and my nephew. After I moved upstairs, I got a job at a local dental office in the front office as receptionist. I was hired because I had a medical background. They were nice dentists and close by. I got to spend time with those I love, and work too, although it was still not a career I wanted.

Linda met a lady across the street, Mrs. Stockey. She was an old Polish lady with no car and she walked everywhere. Upstairs from her was a woman named Dorothy who befriended Linda as she had a little girl the same age as Jim and they would play. Dorothy liked to party. She was divorced and had a friend named Ron whom she'd dated in high school. He was clearly infatuated with her. He was fun and a good person. Between Dorothy and Ron, the parties were never dull. Allen became my partner in crime. Linda was so controlling in the money department (because she had to be), Allen and I would sometimes buy something we liked and sneak it by her. We also decided to take tennis lessons and really enjoyed that. He was a good tennis player and I had a monster backhand; forehand not so good. But we enjoyed playing together. He was also a runner and liked running but his real love was music. He had a huge music collection and saw Bob Dylan whenever he could. He could just zone out when listening to music, much to Linda's dismay as he sometimes didn't hear Jim.

The dentists were in need of a dental assistant so decided to train me as assistant to their newest dentist. He was a pain in the booty and expected more from me than I was capable of giving. He had high expectations but I really wasn't into assisting, though I tried my best. I had a friend who worked at the local college and would visit her, along with still visiting my friend Polly a few hours away. Polly said our friend Phil, whom we bowled with, was sad that I had left, and felt like he missed his chance with me. I told her I would come down sometime and we could all go out. In the meantime, I applied for a job at the college in the sports department, as one of the secretaries. It was better paying and more exciting than a dental office, though I did appreciate how nice the dental office folks were to me, and it gave me experience I would need later.

My nephew was challenging to say the least. Little Jim, once he found his voice, never stopped and once he could walk, he ran. It was hard to keep up with him, and he knew it. He was also smart. I remember going to a grocery store with them and Linda saw a lady coming at us from the other end of the aisle, she couldn't turn around fast enough before Jim said "Boy, Mommy, that lady is fat!" He got a chuckle out of our reactions. We took off fast out of that store. Linda usually had an opinion about everything and even though sometimes she didn't voice it, Jim never gave her the benefit of the doubt. So, like his mother, little Jim eventually kept a lot of his true feelings to himself. But he knew he was loved beyond a shadow of a doubt. Linda never kept those feelings to herself. We had a lot of fun times and I enjoyed being with them for the holidays. It's such a blessing to watch a young child light up like the twinkling lights at Christmas. I would wake up before Jim got up, just to be there to see the look on his face when he saw Santa had come. Those were precious moments to me. Linda kept up our family tradition of going all out for Christmas and she was also a great cook.

When Jim was about six, Grandmommy would watch him some afternoons. Linda got a part time job in the library at the local college, and of course, met friends there also. I remember someone telling me later on, if Linda wanted to be friends with you, you had no option. Linda would call Mom and tell her Jim was coming and Grandmommy would go wait for him so she could cross the road with him. He loved being with his grandmother and Goldie. Jim had a soft side for animals, especially dogs. I think he loved dogs better than people, and this would continue as he grew older. I think he understood them and cherished their unconditional love.

True to my word, I went to see Polly and to have a date with Phil. We had dinner at Polly's and played cards. He was divorced and older than me, quiet and reserved with a good sense of humor. I went back home the next day and Phil promised to visit me. He would come up for the day on the weekends and drive back home. This went on for a while. He met Mom and Linda, and Allen liked him. He tried to teach me to play golf and decided I needed the basics from a pro. I'm glad I did. I bought my own clubs and when Phil came up, we sometimes played. I loved competitive sports, whether playing against myself or others and golf was a challenge to me. That little white ball usually won.

We liked to play cards. Allen had no use for that, so it was just Phil and I, my sister Linda and sometimes neighbors of Linda and Allen's, and none of us ever wanted to lose. We pretended not to care, but each one of us was very competitive. It was on one of those visits, when a blizzard snowed us in, that Phil and I decided to give it a go and get married. My family liked Phil. He was pretty easy going which is the side he chose to show them. We planned our wedding, invited a few people and arranged to have it at Mom's. We decided to get married on April 1 as we both felt we were fools to do this again. Polly's husband Ben was Phil's best man and my sister was my maid of honor. Uncle George was going to perform the ceremony, but he told me it was the last time he would marry me! We had a good time cooking all the food and seeing people we hadn't seen in a long while like Mom's old neighbors and our cousins from the south and friends. We got married to Judy Collins singing "Send in the Clowns."

Not an auspicious start to a marriage. I guess a small part of both of us expected it would be doomed. Nevertheless, we drove down south for a golfing honeymoon. It was the first chance for me to see another side of Phil. He didn't want to go out to eat when we were there. He just wanted to stay in the room and watch TV and relax. But I was raring to go. I guess he was tired. He did love to play golf, so eventually we did a lot of that, on a championship course. But that little voice in me had started a small chatter.

I moved into his apartment in Connecticut. I got a different job that was closer to our apartment, in a huge dental office as a billing clerk. I met a lot of nice people, some of whom are friends for over 30 years now. Missy was a dental assistant and we became friends. She lived not far from us and had an apartment with her sister, and not too far from her mother, older sister, and brother. My other friend, Barbara, worked in the lab fixing partials and prepping teeth for the prosthetics lab.

Life with Phil continued on. We both worked and on weekends and at night we played golf. We joined a local club with Polly and Ben and played in leagues. I still wasn't that good but I really enjoyed playing. We also liked to bat around a tennis ball. We took some vacations and still continued to go and see Mom and my sister. His father had a place in Florida and his mother had an apartment not far from us, as well as his brother. We didn't see much of them. Once again, I was in a relationship where I submerged my own personality for another's. He liked elevator music and couldn't stand me playing the rock and roll and classics that I liked, so I didn't listen to my precious music. Phil didn't talk about feelings or anything related to them. If he wanted to argue about something, he would clam up and not talk, for weeks at a time. He felt it was better not to talk than to put things out there and resolve them. The worst part was that he thought he knew what I was thinking, which for me was completely contrary to what I was actually thinking. I was amazed someone could be like that. I felt he had no trust or respect for me.

Eventually he would talk. It was one of those times that I was home, hiding in a bedroom and I didn't answer any calls. My friend Polly banged on our door and said she was trying to get a hold of us, that Uncle George had passed. I was heartbroken. He was such a dear man. He had had heart problems and was doing rehab but I guess it wasn't enough. Again, I attended another memorial service which took a part of my spirit. That part of the family was gone; my grandfather, my Dad and my uncle. Our close family was shrinking. Occasionally my friend Missy would come to stay with us. My sister and Allen had taken up cross country skiing and we all enjoyed going to the different parks that offered it. Ron, Dorothy's husband, would come with us. Sometimes we would ski in a different area and our lab friend Barbara would join us. We would always pack a lunch as it was very labor intensive but a nice quiet place to be in the Winter. I remember once on a particularly arduous trail Barbara fell and couldn't get up. She had broken her arm. We all felt so bad. We got her to a hospital; it would take a long time to heal and it would be the end of skiing for her. She was 17 years older than I, and I was impressed at all she did in her life. She was always unstoppable, and you never knew what would fly out of her mouth. She liked to say outrageous things and see your expression.

One of the times Missy came with us, we skied during the day and had a wonderful dinner and played cards with neighbors Dorothy and Ron. We had a good time, drinking and laughing. I never saw the warning signs from Phil; He never liked parties and if he thought things were getting out of hand, he wanted to go. Well, I didn't. The next thing I knew, he was gone. He had driven back home and left Missy and I there with no way to get back to our jobs the next day. Well, Ron worked close by, so he said he would take us home the next day on his way to work, which is what happened. I was so furious and of course, Phil wouldn't talk about it. I think that silence went on for weeks. I was just angry and hurt.

It was through Polly, that we met another friend, Jeanne. She was a real estate broker and slower than molasses. If you wanted to go anywhere with her, you told her a half hour earlier than the real time. She was a kind, sweet woman so you could never be mad at her. Phil and I sometimes played tennis with her on New Year's Eve, which was a blast. We enjoyed doing that much more than a crowded party. We decided we wanted to buy a house. In the back of my mind, I wondered if this was good idea as I had that spark of intuition telling me not to put roots down with him. I didn't listen. We went in search of a house with Jeanne. Jeanne was a lovely lady. She always did her homework and lined up houses for us to see, but it was a frustrating journey. She never remembered where she was going and drove Really Slow and never stopped chatting the whole time. It was a real trip, one which we both laughed about at the end of the day, not while it was happening.

We eventually found a house on the hill way out in the country. It was a raised ranch with a lot of land for Phil to have a garden. It wasn't too far from work for both of us. There was also a pond nearby and Phil liked to fish. We had a nice little deck off the kitchen that looked out into the substantial back yard. It was a little piece of heaven for me because I could have bird feeders. I loved to watch the birds and their activity and see how many different ones I could bring to the feeders. I have continually loved to watch birds. To me, they are little messengers from another world. Maybe because of my love for non-human companions, we decided to rescue a puppy. He was a cross between a lab and a hot dog. He was funny looking but a real precious boy who was afraid of the wind. I remember when Linda and Allen came to visit, he went screaming into the garage because he saw some new faces. He would eventually come around. Phil named him Jax. He refused to confine him at all while we were working, so I would come home and find toilet paper strewn from wall to wall along with whatever else he could find. I would just go out and sit on the deck until Phil came home and let him clean it up. Aside from Mom's Goldie, I had never had a dog before, only cats and birds. I would never be without a dog again though! We also adopted a cat named sooty. He got his name when he was very small and we lost him in the heating ducts. He was black but any little white he had on him was covered in soot. He was part Siamese and I loved him. He liked to eat dog food as well as his own food. If not consciously, I intuitively knew, animals were a respite from the lack of love I felt in my marriage.

Work was really hard on me, I felt I had to do it all. The manager found a computer system for the office and I was in charge of loading everything on it and learning everything about it. It took a while to realize, I had to ask for help, that I couldn't do it all myself. I did eventually learn the system and we got it up and running. I heard the computer company was looking for a training person for their system. It was a relatively new company and growing faster than the employees could handle. Phil and I were distancing ourselves from each other. I was sleeping in the spare bedroom. I took the computer training job, but only had to travel to the main office once in a while for training. I maintained an office in the present dental office as it benefited them. The job involved travel and this is when I started flying all over the place. The service people were supposed to get there a day ahead of me to have everything ready, but nine times out of ten, there was something wrong. I managed though and found my little niche. I enjoyed traveling and meeting new people. I had a good work ethic and most times hit the ground running as soon as the plane landed and sometimes didn't get back to the hotel until after six. I was challenging myself. I was at a training session in Washington, DC when the Challenger disaster happened in January of 1986. I remember the horror of it all. The poor students and family of that teacher from New Hampshire, and of course, all the other families. We had never witnessed anything like that before.

You have many acquaintances in your life, but only a few friends. I stayed friends with Missy and Barbara once I left the dental office, also Polly and Connie though we didn't stay in close touch all those years. However, we were close in our hearts.

After eight years, Phil and I decided to split. It was mutual, since we were really living separate lives. I think he was surprised though that I wasn't going to fight with him over anything. I didn't want to go through a big court scene like the last one, so we agreed he would refinance the house and give me the equity money. I just left. Curtain down! The hardest part was leaving the cat and dog, but I knew they would be happier in the home they always knew.

I got an apartment on my own. My friend Polly was very upset and she thought I should stay, but my friends never knew the whole story as I never spoke of the true nature of the marriage. Missy had an inkling, for she had a taste of the real world. I would rather get things out in the open so they could be resolved, or not. Most of the issues were not resolvable anyway. Any man knows they don't know what a woman is thinking. One can never know what another is thinking and it's none of their business anyway!

I continued to work for the dental computer company but was getting sick of all the traveling and was becoming less enamored of the company. One of our customers had just put in the computer system in his office and he said he was looking for an office manager. I told him I was available and so started another experience. I quit my job and went to work for a couple of dentists. They were relatively young and had a good sense of humor. Barry was all about collecting money owed to the practice and I was told to set up a plan to do so. I did, but it sure raised a fuss with all the patients who were used to just paying when they wanted. It was a complete change for the practice and I'm sure some left. It was a time of learning for me—learning how to be a boss. I can say, I wasn't a very good one. I have since learned you get more with honey than vinegar. The other partner, Ted, was the complete opposite. We got along well and eventually started a relationship. I think I took him out of his comfort zone and he liked hiding the relationship from Barry and the rest of the office, and of course, having some fun. It was great for me because he was the complete opposite of what I had known before. He was loving and funny and not serious at all. We started the relationship with no strings attached but both of us got caught up in each other. We went to concerts and traded funny inappropriate Christmas cards and gifts because we both had the same sense of humor and really enjoyed each other. Then Barry told him to put the Kibosh on it, which he did as he wanted to continue being a partner in that practice. I'm sure Barry thought I would not treat them equally if I was enamored with Ted. I never understood why Ted became so aloof, but eventually figured it out. I know he was hurt and so was I. On the other hand, he should have had the gumption to stick up for what he wanted.

I had a few different relationships while I lived in that apartment. One with an insurance salesman, and one with a car salesman/don't know what. He was always secretive. I met him on line and he was the complete opposite of someone I usually chose. Big and fun. I was always looking for someone to fill the void in my life and met another man through an online dating service. There was something funny about him also. I was in a pattern of choosing men who would not live up to my expectations, or were manipulative.

I eventually left that practice and the dental field all together deciding that dentists were a crazy bunch. I went to work in a local hospital in the transcription department again. I would still see my friends, Missy, Polly, Connie and Barbara. We still skied when we had snow. There was something wonderful about being in the woods in winter with no one around. No noise, just peace. I kept going to see Mom and Linda. Linda and Allen bought a single-family home with a huge pool. They were very happy there and Jim was a fish. He still was friends with Dorothy's daughter and Dorothy had married Ron and they didn't live far from the new house. Linda also babysat the daughter of a girl she met at the college. Diane's daughter Kathy was just a baby. Diane needed to work and Linda loved taking care of children, one of the joys of her life. Jim had already taken swimming lessons at the Y and so had Dorothy's daughter but Linda still kept an eye on them in the pool. It gave her time also to sit in the sun with them. Dorothy was very good friends with Linda but when she and Ron decided to split, she told Linda it was her or Ron, no in between. Linda and Allen chose Ron. It was a good choice. He was a kind man and good with Jim and a good friend to Allen. Allen decided he didn't want to ski any longer because he kept really hurting himself when he fell. Linda on the other hand, could go down a hill in slow motion. I never saw anyone control her skis like her. I was a freight train out of control. We kept skiing with Ron and had some good laughs, one time getting stuck in the snow and having to shovel him out and having to pee so bad we almost didn't make it for the laughing we did.

Ron introduced me to his friend Jack who was married but not happy; here we go again, I thought. Jack began skiing with us. Ron had gone to school and grown up with him. Clearly Ron was trying to fix us up. He didn't have much to do because we really took to each other, especially in a spiritual sense. He was interested in a lot of the subjects I was interested in, and had left behind. Native American history, music, hiking, and he introduced me to biking. He came down to my apartment a few times and we just stayed up forever talking and getting to know each other. He was into sports, so during the summer he was busy all the time. But we still had time to take a week in Maine right on a lake. It was hard for him to just relax, but he did. We hiked and talked and carried on and it was blissful. We also took a weekend for skiing in northern Maine with Linda, Ron, Allen and Missy and had a great weekend in a home we had rented. It was so cold, when Missy and I went to the bathroom we couldn't feel our butts. It was definitely one of the coldest weekends ever, but we had good food, good company, and lots of fun. Allen stayed in the camp and read and listened to music. Jack eventually got an apartment close to where he needed to be for his job and his sports. I would come up on the weekend and we would bike all over the place. (First time in my life I didn't have cellulite!) He was a calming influence for me, a Libra like Dad, who listened to me. He would get up before me and bring me coffee in bed, just the way I liked it. I felt we were totally compatible and fell in love. My family liked him and we spent a good part of the time with them too.

It was around this period of time that Linda developed breast cancer. Her PA and good friend Kathy found it. We were devastated and it was the first time we started thinking about our own mortality, and we were so afraid we would lose her. Missy and I had been reading Louise Hay's book, *You can heal your life*. We loved her teachings, and knew that she had cured her own cancer. She also introduced us to Bernie Siegal who was a surgeon who had kept delivering bad news to his patients till they decided not to listen and kept living in spite of his advice. He wrote a book about that. I remember Louise Hay telling a story about a pocketbook that someone had given her and she didn't want such a summer bag because she may not be there in the Spring. But she was. Again, it was a message about believing and trusting and healing. I was brought up loosely in the Protestant faith. I never had any use for organized religion. I would see folks going to church on Sunday and holidays and then turn around and be mean and nasty to each other. It just didn't fit. I always maintained hope as a priority in my life, even when there was none. I was starting to realize just what I believed in. I can remember listening to "A Bridge Over Troubled Waters" by Simon and Garfunkel when I was about 8. I listened to that song over and over until Mom wanted to break it, but the words resonated deep in my soul, although at that young age I didn't realize it.

Linda had a malignant cancer and decided to have a mastectomy. Her chances were good. While she was in the hospital, I brought her a summer pocketbook. She understood immediately why I brought it to her and saved it for the summer. It was the time when AIDS was ravaging young men and there was no cure. Louise and Bernie did a lot of work with the gay community and we went to a lecture they were having in Boston. Missy's sister lived there, so we all piled into the car. After the lecture, Bernie and Louise came out into the audience and we all held hands. Bernie grabbed Linda's hand. It was a first instance of synchronicity, though I wouldn't know it at the time. We all just looked at each other with amazement in our eyes. I'm not sure how much her son Jim understood all that was going on. He kept to himself. To this day, I'm never sure what he's thinking or feeling, quite a bit like his Mom. Linda always wanted to protect him. She always said to him when he went out, be careful, you're all I've got.

It was at this point that I decided I wanted to be closer to my sister so I decided to get an apartment in a town or so over from them. I talked it over with Jack and he seemed to think it was a good idea. I was to move in October. I remember going to Jack's apartment one weekend, when he knew I was coming. I had all his birthday presents, but he wasn't there. He didn't have a cell phone back then so I just left a note for him to call me and left the gifts. He never did. I always figured I scared him off by wanting to move closer to him, but then later in life, I realized he just wasn't emotionally available. I was crushed. I knew he was the one, the one person I could be myself with, no criticism, just love, understanding and friendship. How could I not see this coming? With all of my explorations into spiritual knowledge I didn't listen to my own intuition. But funnily enough, I hear that from everyone who is intuitive. You are too close to the situation to see and feel an answer or the guidance that is right there. That set me backwards to where I felt unworthy of a loving relationship. I never realized until much later, how much my upbringing had affected my psyche.

7

Moving On

I continued working and living in my new apartment, which was actually an old home and an older couple owned it and lived downstairs. They were the sweetest couple. I continued riding my bike past the farm lands and one time stopped as I saw some cows in a small pen and realized one of them was giving birth. I was panicked, realizing that no-one was there to help her! I just watched for a while to see if she was okay. I would discover later that that was the birthing pen they were in and that they didn't need any help. It was glorious to be able to see that and to be outside on my bike. It felt so freeing to ride. I felt an emptiness in my life with Jack disappearing, so not having learned from past mistakes, I answered an ad in an online dating site.

I went out to coffee with Bill. He was adventurous and worked and sold boats on the side. It was winter and we went to see his boat that was in a winterized slip nearby. It was huge to me. He had a dog named Jake that went everywhere with him and Jake liked me. I guess that was the clincher for Bill. If the dog liked me, then he did. We started dating. We would meet some of his friends, have pizza, spend time at home and when winter was over, take the boat out. It was the first time I was introduced to boating and I loved being on the water. It was a 34-footer so we could sleep on it. People with large boats would stay on their boats on the weekend and go out during the day and party at night. Bill was a fisherman and his dream was to rig up his boat for deep sea fishing and take people out to catch big fish. I met his parents and family. I loved his dad, though his mom was a little scary. She had a heavy energy. Bill met my sister and Allen and Mom. They were very non-committal about their feelings about him. He liked to talk about himself. He would listen to others, but it never seemed to matter what was said unless it had a connection to him. He had attended an elite college and had been married before, although when he was much younger.

He was controlling, I would soon find out. He also belonged to Mensa, the notable high IQ society. He used that sometimes as an excuse, in other words, that he couldn't help it if he was so smart. I was still in the mode of needing to have a man in my life, so I put him above me. He could be very charming when he wanted to be and very funny. He knew how to manipulate people. Well, every day problem solving wasn't his best suit when things didn't go his way. He worked as a manager in manufacturing company and after work and weekends sold boats. He finally realized his dream and got a boat slip way up North and so had to hire someone to move his boat. He finally found someone and was crunched for time as the guy didn't show up on time and the law said that the boat and trailer had to be off the highway by sunset. Well, that was no problem, because the trailer broke down in a rest area, so we had to stay overnight a bit farther down than we were supposed to be. We found a place we could launch the boat and stay overnight and then leave early in the morning and drive the boat up to where we were supposed to be. Bill let Jake have his freedom even though he was 4 with a mind of his own, and when it came time to leave, he couldn't find him and he didn't come when called. We had to stay there until Jake decided to arrive. I couldn't believe he would let the dog wander in a place he was unfamiliar with but he obviously didn't see the dangers. It was pretty scary driving the boat in a place we didn't know with only maps to guide us as we hadn't put on radar or anything yet, just a depth finder. I did love being out on the water though and we eventually arrived at the dock where he had paid for a slip.

There were a couple of other locals who had fishing boats there and did charters out of there. One, whom we met, was John who drank a lot and carried on, as most of them did. A real good ole local boy. Well, none of them appreciated Mr. City boy who thought he knew everything. They had his number pretty quickly and pretended to get along. When he went out to fish the first time, they told him where to go and how deep it was where the fish were. Well, they set him up and he almost grounded the boat, before he realized the bottom came up pretty fast and it was not where they said it was. He then had an inkling that he couldn't trust the locals. They got a good laugh out of that one. He had downriggers and was learning this type of fishing himself. Bill was used to stream fishing in waders. He wanted to be a charter captain and take people out fishing, so he set out to get his captain's license which took two tries before he passed. It was four hours to drive home on a Sunday night and then work a full week at our regular jobs. I didn't like living on my own and I liked adventure so I eventually moved in with Bill.

He was still working and selling boats too, and I went to pick him up to go to Linda's for Allen's birthday. I drove into the marina that hot day in August and didn't see Jake running around, since he just let him roam while he worked inside. I parked next to Bill's car and looked in. There was Jake lying in the back seat with the windows closed. I went screaming into the marina to find Bill and tell him that Jake was in a hot car with the windows shut. He came running out and opened the car but Jake was gone. I will never forget how horrified I was to see that loving dog dead. Bill went wild, put him in the water to try and revive him but it was way too late. He was screaming at the top of his lungs, who killed my dog? Well, apparently it started raining and Jake ran up to the car and some kids let him in but never thought to let him out again. I will remember that as long as I live.

In my mind, Bill was the one who was responsible. To me, a dog is like a two-year-old child, and you wouldn't let a two- year-old wander alone. We never went to Linda's. We went home and he buried Jake. He was crying and mad and tearful and I like to think deep down, he knew it was partly his fault, although that ego of his was very self-protective. Bill ended up getting a new car as he couldn't bear to drive the death car anymore. It was a huge loss for him as he felt Jake was a part of him and he even took him to work with him. Everyone knew Jake. I still get sick to my stomach when I think of the poor little guy.

Several months later, he came home late one day and said he had been to the dog pound and saw a little dog there and would I go with him to see him. Here was this little guy just staring through the bars at us. He was probably four years old or so, and weighed about 20 pounds. He looked to be a terrier/beagle mix. We took him home. It took a while to get him trained as Bill kept comparing him to Jake who was well trained, according to Bill. He was strict with him, and the dog loved him all the more. He would go with us to the boat on Friday nights and loved being on the boat. We named him Chinook after the fish in the lake. He was a big fish also, in personality. Eventually he figured out what we were doing and used to sit on the fly bridge and watch the downriggers. He would start whining just before a fish would hit and then didn't stop barking until we brought the fish in the boat and if you let him near it, he would try to bite it. Funny dog. Everyone on the lake could hear him barking and knew when we had a fish and would call and ask where we were.

Yes, Bill figured out how to fish and was pretty good at it. He started taking bookings and almost never came back without fish. He was not nice to me, as I had to direct the customers and tell him which way to turn the boat. He would yell that I didn't tell him which way to turn the boat, or I didn't watch the downriggers and it was constant, so much so that the customers would be looking at each other and wondering why I was even there. He would come flying down the ladder to the fly bridge and take rods out of my hand and tell me to go up and steer the boat. He was always right, because he was so intelligent. He always used light line so the fish would put up a good fight and if it was a big fish, we had to tire it out with the boat. It was exciting as salmon just took the line and ran. It would sometimes take an hour to bring in a huge fish but that's what the customers wanted. They loved it. He became friends with a couple of charter fisherman. One was a college grad like him, Robert, and had a camp on the lake. Once in a while we would go there for a picnic when we didn't have a charter or it rained so hard, we couldn't go out. In his stuffiness, Bill could relate to Robert because he was a college grad and not a local. Most of the locals did strictly bass fishing and paid him no mind. We never really had time to do that unless the weather was bad, the boat was being repaired, or someone cancelled at the last minute. But we never really got a chance to enjoy the boat ourselves once he started doing charters.

I was almost forty when I realized I was pregnant. I had been told I would never have a child because of the scar tissue from my abortion years ago, so I was surprised. So was Bill! He was happy though and so was I, to have a second chance. Bill expected me to continue being first mate and travel and work on the boat and travel home again, even though I would have cramping and minor bleeding. He was always verbally pushy, and later I would learn, no-one really liked him. He thought it would be better for me and the baby to get regular exercise but I know he was only thinking of himself.

Mom and Linda were so excited and started buying baby things. I had an ultrasound and knew it was a boy. They wanted me to have amniocentesis at twenty weeks since I was older. I had just started to feel movement and the love for the baby grew and we started planning. I went in for the amniocentesis by myself as Bill was working. I saw the face of the tech doing the ultrasound before the procedure and she left the room and came back with the doctor. They couldn't find a heartbeat. There was no need for the amniocentesis. I called Bill and he came running. He was as devastated as I was. He then told me how he was going to build a crib and other furniture and how he knew I would have been a wonderful mother. The only kind words I would hear from him.

We both thought it was payback for us both having prior abortions. He had his ex-wife get an abortion because he wasn't ready for a child. Cause and effect. I had to carry our child until the scheduled delivery. Since I was twenty weeks, I had to go into labor and have the baby. I did get to hold him and sent him away with my love. Meanwhile Mom and Linda had come to the house and removed all baby stuff. It was another horrible time in my life and one for which I felt responsible. My heart was broken. Again. Apparently, there was a chromosome problem, he was missing one. Knowing there was a genetic problem did not help my pain. This would not be the end of my son though, and not the worst time of my life, which was still to come.

One would think writing all this down would be cathartic, but it has the opposite effect. I have to take breaks as the tears flow in concert with the memories. It would all make sense eventually, but right then, I wish my blocking mechanism would kick in, but the curtain didn't fall and it doesn't any longer. I've learned we need to take in our grief and absorb it before we can heal and move on.

Bill and I decided to keep trying for another child. We even tried invitro but it became too much for us with our lives on a schedule of shots and sex. We both decided we had had enough and stopped trying. We were busy with our multiple jobs, working forty hours and spending Friday night till Sunday night with our charters. We decided matter-of-factly to get married since we were already acting that way. One weekend we had a justice of the peace come to the house and marry us. I had already bought and paid for a ring for myself. How pitiful is that! When I went to work on Monday, my coworkers asked me what the ring was and I told them I got married that weekend. They were shocked that I was so nonchalant about it.

Bill decided to get another dog and brought home an English Springer Spaniel and named her Coco. She was a spastic dog and loved catching a ball until she held it in her mouth and lay down to rest and then was ready to go again. Chinook had no place in his life for another dog as he was head honcho. One day he led her out into the road to try and ditch her but Bill caught him. We had woods in the back and that was another way Chinook tried to ditch her. He took her out there and he came back and she didn't. She was a flake and couldn't find her way out of a basket. But in time, she found her way home. She was not good on the boat either, I think she got seasick. She didn't enjoy it like Chinook did. I was against another dog and later on, I thought Bill wanted to get Coco for me so I wouldn't be so attached to Chinook.

His college reunion was coming up on a Saturday night, so he decided to go to the boat and from there go to his reunion. I had no desire to go and had to work anyway. So, I packed his boat clothes and his party clothes and off he went. I kept the dogs because they would be in the way with just one of us there. He came back late Sunday night, saying he caught up with some old friends and had a good time. That night, we went out to eat with some friends and he talked a little about the reunion and we joked about me packing his good clothes and his fishing clothes and I remember the funny look on his face when I was talking. I wondered what he was thinking as it was an odd look. (Intuition kicking in). Well, I found out the following Friday when I came home from work, ready to roll up to the lake and found a note on the kitchen table from Bill. (He had horrible penmanship for someone so smart!) But he got his point across that he thought we had come to the end of the line, that I was a wonderful person but he needed to go in a different direction. There was more, but I couldn't remember. He had left work early, got his stuff and the dogs and left for the boat.

I was flabbergasted. I never saw that coming either. Our marriage was never perfect but I had settled into it. He never came home. Some of his childhood friends were customers that weekend and I had a good relationship with them. I called them. They said that Bill had reconnected with an old classmate of his and she was on the boat with him. They tried to make me feel better, saying she was a dog but now the story came out. We had both said to each other that we would never cheat on each other, so he just left before he did. I was furious. Plus, he had my dog. He wouldn't answer calls. I had no idea where he was. I would stalk where he played hockey and one time saw her with him. After he decided I had cooled down, he came over with a pizza knowing it was my favorite food, and wanted to talk. I wasn't fooled. I told him to take his pizza and get out I was so mad, I'm sure my cop neighbor, who had become a friend, heard all the screaming.

One day I came home and Bill had broken a window in the basement and came in the house to take a few things including a painting we had commissioned on our honeymoon. It was just to prove to me that he could come and go whenever he wanted. Well, I freaked out. I talked to the cop next door and we got a restraining order. He knew how upset and afraid I was. I also hired a female lawyer someone recommended. She was a doll. I gave her the note and she had Bill's number and knew exactly how to handle things. She knew he would take his big fat foot and put it in his mouth and piss off a judge. So, we put plans in place. But I wanted my dog. I was afraid the same thing would happen to him as Jake. I went to visit Linda with a plan in mind. Even though I had a restraining order against him, I still had keys to his car and he played hockey in the same town as my sister. I knew he was living in a tent and he had to take the dogs with him. I went to the rink and I got Chinook and took him to my sisters and left Coco. I knew he wouldn't try to break in and take him because he obeyed the law. Of course, he took me to court and complained but all the judge did was take the keys away.

Okay. One up on Mr. Smarty pants. He underestimated me. True to my lawyer's characterization of Bill, she sat back and let him cook his goose. He got a separate lawyer that had won a dog case before but all in all, the judge said, you have a dog, she has a dog, get on with it. And that was that. He had to put money down on a house for me and he got his house back. I moved about a mile from Linda and still commuted back and forth to work. End of Bill, so to speak, until later. Remember, they all come back in one form or another until the lesson is complete.

8

Travels and Adventures

My house was an old Victorian. I loved it. I fenced in the small yard for Chinook. It needed some work but I could do that piecemeal. The first thing I did was pull up the orange shag carpet which had been down for eons. It was gross and there was beautiful hardwood beneath it without a mark on it. That took a while and the process was dusty and dirty but I eventually got it done. I pulled out all the nails and cleaned and polished the floor and what a difference it made. The day I moved in though, I was standing in the kitchen and apparently someone had flushed the upstairs toilet as water started streaming from the kitchen overhead light. Yikes. Luckily my good friends, Barbara and her husband Leland, were there to help solve my problem. Leland was also good at making shelves in closets which had none! They were a godsend. All the bedrooms were upstairs and mine had a bench seat cupboard. That was Chinook's. He loved sitting up there and looking out the window and barking at mailmen, UPS guys and kids on skateboards, all of which drove him nuts! If I left to go to work, I'd look at that bedroom and there he would be, sitting in the window and he'd come running down the stairs as soon as I drove in. The house had a huge barn/garage but the garage door opener didn't work and they had never used it as a garage. Well, I didn't want to keep my car outside so I got a book and a spare part and I fixed that damn thing myself. You would have thought I did brain surgery. My first inkling of self-sufficiency! I also started going to a counselor.

I knew after the marriage with Bill that I didn't want to repeat any of my prior relationships. Little did I know, all of the men in my life came back in one form or another; I guess to see if I "got" the lesson involved. Even if you're intuitive, it's very hard to listen to that little voice when your ego, that's been telling you who you are for your whole life, gets in the way. Time for a new start all around. Just me and Chinook. We were close to Linda and Mother, and life was good except for the commute. Our sister hospital in the same town had an opening for a transcriptionist, so I jumped at it and started working in my town. This is where most of my medical knowledge came from, learning medical transcription rather than Radiology. There's a big difference, especially when transcribing surgeries. After a while, I felt like I could do one myself! I ended up becoming the lead transcriptionist.

Linda discovered computers and was driving herself crazy learning to use the mouse. She thought she would never get it. It was laughable. All of her early marriage, she saved and actually made money through couponing. There were three grocery stores in our town and she would look at the sales, get a coupon for what she wanted and ended up paying nothing. Even if she didn't want the product, she saved it to trade. She met a lovely lady on line, Jean who lived a few hours away, and they traded coupons and talked via email. Eventually Jean came for a visit and we all became friends. She was funny and could really talk, but she was really smart about retail. Jean introduced Linda to selling on eBay. Once that began, she got the bug and became a real shopper. She had survived her breast cancer and was doing volunteer work for "reach for recovery" with other breast cancer patients. Linda always gave back in any way she could. Jim was in his early twenties, trying to decide what to do with his life. He was working part time stocking shelves at a local grocery store and going to college. Allen was teaching at the local middle school.

Occasionally, I got invited by friends to spend the weekend back at the lake. It was fun for a while but I was really tired of that hike, although one time it was a pleasure to see Bill's face when he noticed me on another boat having a good time. He always underestimated me and the people that liked me and didn't like him. Oh yes, I was told quite a few times how no-one liked him, including my family. I guess I probably wouldn't have listened if they told me. We all have lessons in life we need to learn, even though they may seem impossible at the time. My time with Bill happened to be an important lesson, in more ways than one.

I would do a lot of shopping with Linda looking for eBay prizes. She could spend hours in one store, especially the Christmas Tree Shop, but she would find things I never saw! She had a good sense of what sold and what didn't, but sometimes she got stuck with things. Once she sold something for a good price and made money, she'd buy ten more and usually got stuck with some of them. Up into the attic they would go. She always stockpiled for gifts also. You never knew when you would need something for someone. She loved to give and make people happy. If she knew you liked something, she would keep her eyes out for it, especially if it were on sale. She would then save it for an opportune moment. Some people didn't understand this about her. They didn't see the real Linda, and thought she was trying to buy your love or friendship, or whatever. That was so far from the truth; she got absolute joy in giving and finding the perfect gift. As an example, when we were very young, at Christmas time, we used to listen to the record "The Littlest Angel" by Loretta Young. At some point, my parents loaned it to someone and we never got it back. I absolutely cherished that memory and I guess I resonated with angels even back then. Well Linda searched the internet and found the old record plus a CD of the original recording and she gave it to me for Christmas one year.

I was absolutely gabber smacked that she found it! She— who didn't even know how to use a mouse to begin with. That was how resolute she was when she wanted to find something special for someone. I was overcome with emotion and love.

I was still friends with Missy from the dental office, and once in a while would drive to the city to see her sister. I remember one such jaunt, drinking a bottle of wine along the way. We were two peas in a pod, always happy and always adventurous. We decided to take a trip to Sedona because we wanted to experience the ley lines, or as some called them, vortices. We ended up flying into Albuquerque, but my luggage didn't arrive with me and they had given away our rental car! We looked out of our hotel window and there was a hot air balloon. This was October, and we never knew it was the hot air balloon festival which is why so many people were there. The next day my luggage arrived and we rented a car from a local garage and took off in the early morning for Arizona. It was early and we went by the balloon festival where they were firing up the balloons. I'd never seen so many in my life; the view of them all was magical. On the way to Sedona, we stopped at an Acoma reservation which was the longest inhabited reservation in the country. We took a tour and we each bought a handmade vase by a local. The energy there was awesome and you could look out all over the countryside as it was perched up high in the hills. The residents still cooked and made bread in the rock ovens. It was awe inspiring. We continued on to Sedona, amazed by the red rock formations and could feel almost physically that it was a very spiritual place. Even as we were driving in, Missy and I could feel the vibrational energy throughout our bodies. We stayed at a hotel on one of the rock formations, not far from one of the ley lines. It was our goal on this vacation to visit as many as we could and see if we could feel the vibrations. We also took a helicopter ride which sidled up against the rock dweller formations that were still in place. It was the only way to see them. It was scary/good. We hiked among the red rocks and toured Sedona, loving every minute of it and wanting to retire there, except there was no ocean . . . There was Lake Havasu, but no match for an ocean. We traveled on to the Grand Canyon, or as one would say, the big hole. Everything was flat, so you could drive 100MPH and never know it. To me, the Grand Canyon was really frightening as you could perch right on the edge and there were no railings or anything to prevent someone from falling. I'm afraid of heights, so it was not a favorite part of the trip but certainly something amazing to see.

From there we went to Santa Fe, stopping at a reservation along the way and buying more native items. Of course, we shopped in Santa Fe with the local vendors. The town was so quaint and charming; we loved it there. Unfortunately, we had to get back to New Mexico to catch our flight and turn in the car. We weren't supposed to take it out of state but breaking a little rule was part of our adventurous mindset and the old girl did us well. The whole trip was inspiring. The energy there was so fabulous but neither of us could see ourselves moving far from an ocean, since we were both water signs.

Our friend Barbara had retired from the dental office and she had a house on a lake, so we would visit her there. In the Winter, she would go down south where she had purchased a house. She was a snowbird, traveling back and forth like that for as long as she could. Barbara was very creative and was always gardening and doing crafts. She taught Linda how to use petal porcelain and we would all go to craft shows. I would try a few different crafts, but they were clearly the ones with creative ability, especially Linda, who was an artist in her own right. Her guidance counselor had talked her out of commercial art, saying there was no future in it. It's not right that adults can shut off young people's dreams, rather than encourage them. In any event we would pack up a tent and take off and do craft shows. It was more of a fun thing than making money and it gave us a chance to visit. The crafts were time consuming and we would never make back what we put into it. But it gave us more ideas for what to search for on our shopping travels.

Linda loved going to Cape Cod and always started planning our week visit in January. She would go on VRBO and try and find a cottage to rent. In the beginning, it was just she and I, but sometimes our friend Jean would pop up to shop with us and stay overnight. Linda always cooked ahead of time because she didn't like to spend money going out to eat except to the local fish place which we always hit. Needless to say, the car was loaded when we left for the Cape and when we came home. She loved finding the light houses and taking pictures and just being near the water. We never really beached it, mostly took walks looking for lighthouses and more than anything else, shopping. There were about 13 Christmas Tree Shops on the Cape as that's where the idea was founded. We would hit every one, and every one had different items for sale.

The first former love to show up again was Jack. He stopped in one day to see Linda and Allen. Not sure how I found out, I think it was Ron who told me. In any event, we reconnected. I believe he told me why he wasn't home on his birthday and it obviously didn't mean too much to me if I can't remember it. We started going out here and there again, even to his nephews for a visit. I do remember sitting on my back steps talking to him, and he asked me to marry him. Oh, by the way, he had been told he has a debilitating illness. I thought about it and looked at him and said, "so, what is it you can do for me"? No answer was forthcoming. I can't believe I actually stood up for myself and asked him that. The old me probably would have said, sure! I wondered later on if he proposed to have someone take care of him, or if it was just a delayed response to our loving relationship. Well, that loving relationship was gone. It left when he walked out although there is still the soul connection between us that will never disappear and we talk, even now, some 20 years later, and there is still a place in my heart where he dwells. One lesson learned! You don't need a man in your life to feel whole. I was doing just fine on my own.

There was a guy across the street from me who grew pumpkins for the local fair. They were huge. He had to get many people to help him when it came to be fair time. He used a mixture of his own seeds. I would pop over once in a while and his friend Dan would show up occasionally on his motorcycle. He was a funny likable guy, married, but we enjoyed each other's company. I had another plumbing issue so I asked my neighbor if he knew a plumber and he gave me the name of one. Who would show up on my steps but Dan with his wife, Irene. He was a plumber. He would become a friend and did a lot of plumbing work for me later on. He was a Scorpio and there was an instant twinkle in his eye, like he recognized me from another life and immediately felt at home.

Linda discovered Facebook and found a bunch of her school mates on line. She was especially thrilled to find her friend Karen who had lived not far from us and had been good friends. She was married and had a couple of adult children by then and also was battling her own breast cancer, but hers was much more severe. Her poor husband was scared to death he would lose her. She won that battle after going through stem cell replacement. So, next time we went to the Cape, we needed to find a bigger place.

Karen started meeting us and staying with us at the Cape and having a ball catching up with life and shopping. There was a lot to catch up on. They were never to lose each other again; one good result from social media. We would play cards at night and drink martinis and munch on snacks. These trips were truly a great time. Jean still kept coming to spend the night. We all made some fantastic memories, the kind you cherish with good friends. Others joined us at different points in time, Darlene from Ohio, who was good friends with Karen and we enjoyed her company too, along with Karen's daughter, June. We declared ourselves "The Cape Crew." Eventually we started heading out early in June before the Summer crowds got there. One time, Linda and I went in October for the weekend and Jean joined us. We made a Ouija board out of cut out letters and a bottle cap. It worked just fine. It happened to be the birthday of Jean's grandmother who came through on the board and spelled out her name. Jean was flabbergasted. We hadn't really been keeping up with spirit contact.

My dear Chinook had some lumps in his belly and I found out he had cancer. The vet tried to cut it out but it never really worked. He just started to deteriorate. I would stay home with him, never leaving him alone, and if I did, Linda would look after him. She was so afraid he would pass on her watch and I didn't blame her. She had a little dog named Maggie, who was Chinook's good buddy. She was a fearful little dog and didn't like it when she was left alone. She would howl, even when someone was home and she hadn't heard them. I thought she was so funny. Chinook taught her how to be fierce with the mailman though, as they had a mail slot and no-one was going to use it! They eventually had to get a mail box to keep the dogs from tearing the mail apart. It got so Chinook stopped eating and I would carry him outside to pee, although since he wasn't eating or drinking much, it was not really necessary but he would die before he would do anything in the house and I knew that. My vet knew the end was near but I kept hoping. She went away for the weekend but before she left, she gave me a bunch of vials of pain killer in case he needed them. I sat on the floor with him all night, injecting pain meds into him. I was supposed to go do a craft show, but I couldn't leave him. He just looked at me with those big brown eyes that seemed to say *enough is enough.* I called another vet to come to the house and put him out of his misery. I clearly should have made that decision months ago but I just couldn't. I held him until he breathed his last breath and then I sobbed for hours.

I called Allen but he didn't answer so I went over there and asked him to help me bury Chinook. He was in tears too but came right over and we put him in the garden. I loved that pup so much and he meant so much to me. Eventually I would get over his death, but one day a year later, in December, all of a sudden, I started sobbing again. It was really crazy. The grief just creeped up on me. I remember Allen was helping me do something in the yard and Jim came over to help. He just looked at me out of the corner of his eye wondering if he should say something, but he really couldn't help himself, and came over and gave me a hug and said how sorry he was about Chinook. He loved him too. Jim loved all dogs. He never showed emotion though, unless it was during a traumatic time in his life.

Life continued on for me. Over time, I got more dogs, but none of them could replace Chinook. Even my vet said that. We always have one special one in our life that none can come close to. Ultimately, I stopped with dogs. I had a job back in the city and was learning medical coding. I finally had surgery for a knee problem which was a bear to rehab so I was home doing that and as I went up and down the stairs on my behind, I realized I needed to find a house on one level or at least where I could have a bedroom and bath on the first floor. Mom was in elderly housing. She had a nice little apartment with one bedroom and didn't have to worry about a house any longer. She would take off on Saturday morning and go do tag sales with Allen's mom and then they would have lunch at their favorite place. It was good for her.

I was lucky. I sold my house, just before the market took a dive and bought a bungalow about a mile away in a really nice part of town. I packed everything and labeled it all and the movers arrived. Barbara and Leroy were there to receive the movers while I was at one of the closings, along with Linda and Allen. My new home had a huge bright orange kitchen that looked out onto the fenced back yard. There was a tiny deck where I could fit one chair. The front of the house had a porch with screens the full width of the house and it would be one of my favorite places to sit. As I was running around, I could see the guy across the street, discreetly looking to see who was moving in. We would become good friends. He was an ex- cop so didn't miss a thing, although he was getting up there in years. He had two little Maltese dogs that he and his wife adored. He also had a love for homing pigeons and kept a pigeon coop out back. Allen had painted the rooms that needed it and I painted my bedroom a soothing lavender. I loved it. There was a huge room upstairs the full width of the house and another room off the stairs. Allen thought it would make a great apartment, without a kitchen of course. It had a big dining room, a den and a living room with a fireplace which I converted to a pellet stove as I liked having a blast of heat in the Winter.

Being single, I took on one big project a year to do. I took out a home equity loan and put in a gas boiler and took out the oil tank. That was a project and I got to see my friend Dan quite a bit. Sometimes Linda and I would be sitting on the porch having a cocktail and Dan would join us after he was done for the day. He had an engineer's mind and could always figure out a way to do things, like getting the oil tank out of my old hatchway. He just tied a rope and used a tree to leverage it up. It was crazy. So was he! We always had a good rapport, like we had known each other before in an earlier life. We probably did. We had the same sense of humor. If he wasn't married, things would have been different. There was a definite spark there.

The second love to show up was Phil. He tracked me down through my friends Connie and Nate. She asked if it was okay if he emailed me. I said sure. I had no hard feelings with him, just sadness. After a while, I saw that our relationship had not changed. That was it. I was not going there again. Exit stage left, test two passed.

Life continued very pleasantly for me. I could hop right onto the highway to get to work and at home, I did a lot of gardening. I dug up the whole backyard next to the fence to put in a perennial garden. That was a long process. Just me and my shovel breaking up the grass. It took quite a few tries to get the plants I wanted. I loved getting out in the dirt and gardening and mowing and even weeding. I rarely wore gloves. I sensed it was a good way to ground myself.

I still kept in touch with Dan. He would come over for the odd plumbing project or just to stop in but he actually decided he'd had enough plumbing and went to work for someone else. He had a close friend who bred field spaniels. He knew I was ready for another dog after so many years. I went to dinner at his house one night and met June and Ed and they brought along Georgia, a five-year-old field spaniel. She was liver colored and beautiful. June and Ed were checking me out to see if I would be a good fit for Georgia. They only kept her and her brother out of the litter and Georgia was getting up in age and they wanted to find her a good home with the rule that if I went on vacation, she would go back to them. Or if it didn't work, she would go back to them. They loved her and they were all she knew. I decided that I would take her. They brought her one afternoon with all her toys and food, etc. And they left. She didn't know me from Adam and kept waiting for her Mom and Dad to come back to get her. She was so scared, she peed on the floor. I felt so bad for her and was determined to give her all the love she needed. It wasn't until two or three years later that she accepted me as her other Mom. She was the sweetest girl. In fact, the cop across the street would come over at lunch to let her out but he ended up walking her and named her Sweetie Pie. We all loved her. She was my girl, except when I went on vacation, and then she went back home with Mom and Dad

9

The Black Years

Linda kept shopping and selling on eBay and eventually filled up the attic, basement, and what we would call her eBay room which was across from her computer and it was full of shelves with brand new products. She was crazy; she would just keep buying. One day she called me after I got home from work and told me to bring over my blood pressure machine when I came for supper because she had the biggest headache she ever had in her life. I did and we took it, but her blood pressure was not totally out of range. When we started eating though, all of her food was pushed to one side of the plate and even falling off and she didn't know it. She said it was the headache. I told Allen to take her to the hospital as I thought she was having a stroke. She felt so bad, she said okay. I stayed there and waited to hear from them and to keep their latest dog Daisy company. I was scared. I didn't like what I saw. Being in the medical field, I knew what a stroke looked like. Allen called much later and said she had a cat scan and there was a mass in her brain. I left the dogs and went to the hospital to join him.

They had consulted a neurologist and determined that it was probably a glioblastoma (that word again). Apparently, they grow so fast, you don't have any symptoms until it's too late. I get sick to my stomach just putting this down on paper. I already went through this with Dad and I prayed, *not my sister too*. She is my best friend and I love her to death. We called Jim and gave him the news and he came up. They wanted to operate the next day so they sent her to a larger hospital to see the neurosurgeon there. She was so scared. She didn't know if she wanted surgery and certainly by some surgeon she didn't know. She had been through this before too! I went home and they took her down to the hospital where I worked. I knew I would see her tomorrow when I went down to work. Funny thing though. I called my second cousin who was a physician. His younger brother was a neurosurgeon and I asked Tim to get a hold of George to give us his opinion on surgery. Well, George just happened to be at a conference an hour away. He got the word from Tim and went to the hospital to see Linda. He was a wonderful loving face for her to see and come to find out, he went to medical school with the surgeon who was going to do her surgery. George looked at the x-rays and talked with his friend and it was like old home week which allayed Linda's fears and mine too. Talk about synchronicity! Her surgeon was a very kind man with daughters of his own and explained everything to all of us. It amazed all of us that George just happened to be close by. I found it hard to believe Linda had survived breast cancer only to develop a brain cancer and no, they were not related. The medical establishment also said glioblastomas weren't hereditary but we know different. We let Mom know what was going on but thought it too long of a drive for her to just come and wait until surgery was done. I'm sure it brought back all the memories of what she went through with Dad but she never let it show. She just worried quietly at home. Allen and I waited for the surgery to be done and then Jim came and waited too.

Linda came out of surgery fine and the doctor had told us in the beginning he would get maybe 80% of it without causing neurological damage. He was so concerned that he didn't cut off all her beautiful hair. I guess that came from four women in his household. We saw her in recovery and she was so agitated about the needles stuck in her head which weren't needles at all but the staples. It was very painful and annoying to her. We tried to do things for her but the nurse said she needed to do them herself. The surgeon asked what oncologist we wanted to see. There was only one in that hospital that had dealt with brain tumors before and I didn't like him. I talked it over with the manager of my department and she said she had only heard good things so I suggested they see him, though deep down, I didn't like it. I should have listened to my intuition.

Linda came home and started chemo and then radiation. She seemed to like her Oncology doctor. I set about learning everything I could about Glioblastoma Multiforme IV. I was like a supercharged brain cancer strategist, even though ultimately, it was not in my hands. I could only make suggestions. And it was not a pretty picture. No cure and about 18 months to two-year survival rate. I found an online informational page produced by a doctor with all the newest drugs and experimental trials. Linda started losing her hair in clumps, but refused to shave her head. She was vain about her hair. She never went to a hairdresser and kept it long and colored it herself. I think she thought if she shaved her head, she would be losing the battle. I don't know. Linda never talked about her true feelings. I could only guess.

The seasons changed and it was coming up on the time we always went to the Cape. We had been going to a condo for a couple of years. We decided we would still go. Linda had packed up all the food like she'd always done and made soup for us all. Karen and her daughter would come up and meet us and, of course, Jean. We all had the thought in the back of our minds that this might be the last time we were all at the Cape together. (But it wasn't!) Linda was so upset that I had to carry everything up the deck stairs as she didn't have the energy to help. I didn't mind. We still shopped, though Linda had a hard time focusing and spent a long time in one place in a store. Karen and I would take turns shadowing her. She would get frustrated that she couldn't find her credit card and would stand in line with people in back of her making faces while Karen and I were ready to do battle with them if they said a word! We went to our favorite fish place for dinner one night and Linda broke down crying because nothing tasted good anymore and she couldn't enjoy it. It crushed us to see her suffer. We took a lot of rides and there was especially one place on the bay side that was a marina with a tiny beach, but Linda was always enthralled by the trees going out into the harbor marking the way for boats. We would sit there and just mellow out. We never went too far from a gift shop we loved because they had unique gifts. Linda liked to poke around and look at everything, upstairs and downstairs. It was a happy time but also tense and filled with anxiety at the same time. We so enjoyed being with all our friends. It also gave Allen a break to be by himself, just listening to music and not worrying.

She kept having MRI's every three months and hated them. The noise, the claustrophobic space, and the constant worry about what they would find or not find, and it seemed as though no one could agree on what was really happening. We finally got her to go to Dana Farber Cancer institute. I drove and we actually found our way. The doctors there had her records and x-rays ahead of time. They determined that the tumor was not growing and suggested medication treatment. Linda could have kissed them. Of course, her doctor, didn't really agree, and only knew one way to treat it—and that was with steroids. She would go to the local hospital and have treatments every week. Eventually nothing tasted good to her and her bowels didn't work which really pissed her off. I tried cooking all sorts of foods for her to find something she would enjoy eating. But the only thing she liked was fresh pineapple. She refused to wear "cancer scarves" and took to wearing a cute little knitted hat but with all the steroids, she looked like a bloated grandmother. I'm sure this was a heartache for her more than anything. It got so the local ambulance crew knew her because she started having seizures. I cried when we were in the emergency room and she had a seizure.

This wasn't my sister. My heart couldn't stand the pain of watching her deteriorate but I never showed her my devastation. She knew I was her staunch supporter, urging her to keep fighting. I could not think about the prognosis.

She eventually went to a local nursing home for rehab because she was having trouble walking and getting around. She was also losing her ability to communicate what she wanted. Jim would come up and visit but I really think he was afraid to think about the outcome and preferred to keep himself in the dark. He was living with a very nice girl with a dog and we loved her. She would come up with him and she was very kind to Linda. We dubbed her a keeper.

Jim had graduated with his Master's in education and was teaching at a high school. To think that this quiet boy would be teaching a bunch of high school kids, or teaching at all, was beyond our comprehension, but he knew what he wanted and went after it. He loves teaching and he makes a big difference in his students lives. The staff of the nursing home were very nice. I would make brownies or cookies for them to butter them up and make sure they were kind to Linda. Allen and I would go every day, and of course all her friends came too. Her friend Kathy, her PA who had found her breast cancer, came after work every day too. I would sometimes pick up Mom, because she didn't drive any longer, and bring her to visit Linda. Mom was in another world at this point and time. She was getting older and I was kind of glad she wasn't absorbing all the pain I was, watching as my sister's body betrayed her. I had asked my manager for family leave but family leave only included mothers, fathers, husbands and wives or children, not sisters, so she and her boss told me to just take whatever time I needed.

One weekend I just needed to get away so I went to see Missy near the ocean. She was living there with her husband and dog and I loved to go up there and just see her and be near the water. Apparently, Linda missed me because when I returned and walked into the nursing home she said, "Oh, there's my sister!" I wanted to break down and sob but I kept it in. We had found that her steroid was increased more than when she came home from surgery and the nurse said her oncology doctor increased it. That steroid had such a bad effect on Linda. We eventually took her by ambulance to another neurologic oncologist near the city. Jim brought a book and rode in the back of the ambulance with her. He agreed with us that she didn't need all those steroids but at this point and time, we got the doctor to decrease them but the damage was already done. In my heart, my worst fears about that oncologist were realized and I felt responsible for all her misery. I felt that the doctor was just following what he knew and would not listen to advice or opinions of others who had a different regimen. The steroids he prescribed where much higher than others recommended. I remember praying to anyone that would listen to please take me instead of her, after all, I was alone, and she had a son to take care of and a husband who loved her.

Jim and his girlfriend Hannah came up to visit one weekend in May and told us that they had gotten married. Everyone was so happy. Linda started planning a reception of sorts for them and set the date for June. Of course, I helped her along with all her friends. Everyone brought food and we had the celebration in one of the rooms off the lobby. Her friends Karen came and Diane put a wig on Linda while Karen did her makeup and she felt more like a woman instead of a big steroid blob. Ron had stayed close by through all of this also, as he loved Linda as much as he loved Allen and was a true friend. We had a grand time and Jim's new puppy was the hit of the party. We had a cake and punch and special treats for everyone, even gifts for Jim and Hannah. Linda had a wonderful time, after all, she had always been the one to put on parties and celebrations and loved people. This was in June and Linda was just about to turn 64 in August.

I was fervently trying to find a way to retire at 62. I knew I couldn't afford it unless I could still work part time and my manager was on board with that. The only problem was affording insurance. I did squeak into a low- income health insurance plan, so that was the clincher. I retired in June of 2011 so I could spend my sister's last days with her. Sometimes we'd go outside in the Fall sunshine because there were train tracks next door to the nursing home and Linda loved trains, just something about them. Her favorite Christmas movie was The Polar Express. I knew she was going to transition soon as she was not eating much and couldn't talk and felt very frustrated.

We would have meetings with the rehab staff and nurses every few weeks and she was really not getting rehab any longer as she wasn't going to benefit from it. She couldn't even get out of bed to go to the bathroom. They had to use a Hoyer lift to get her out of bed. I remember I was on the porch waiting for them to hoist her out of bed and the rehab guy came in and said Linda wanted me. She looked at me, hanging in midair, and said "Louise, I can't do this anymore". I responded with, "I know, and I don't want you to". It was like she was trying to fight this thing, just because I was. I will never forget those words. After that, she just calmly gave in. That weekend, Jim and Hannah came up to visit and I remember Linda was so happy to see them and Hannah helping her to eat. She had hospice help now. She would fade in and out of consciousness but we would just sit there with her, either me, or Allen or Ron or Kathy. Whomever came that day. We weren't going to desert her. A few days later on Oct 3, we got a call in the morning and we were told to get there as it would only be a few hours before she was gone. We called Jim and Hannah to get them out of school, and Ron, and tried to get a hold of Kathy so she could get there but we couldn't reach her. Linda was in a room with another lady so they moved her to a private room. She was completely unconscious and didn't know we were there. Poor Mom, I was so upset, I forgot about her until Jim said, "we should get Grandmommy." I went and picked her up. I was so thankful for him. It was a death wait, that's all I could say. We just stayed with

76

her. I had my hand on one foot and Hannah held the other. I could feel the life leave her and I knew when she was gone. I was sobbing and so was Jim, I just grabbed him and held him close. Mom didn't cry. She was just talking about how she was such a tiny little baby. She just couldn't get her head around that she just lost her firstborn. We all left with plans to go to my house and have a drink to toast my sister. We called everyone we needed to, but still couldn't get Kathy and she would end up going to the nursing home that afternoon and getting the news. Allen stayed behind to say his last goodbye before coming over. It was like part of my heart was torn from me. I didn't want to live. I didn't want to be alone. I didn't know what to do with myself. We were like twins because we were so close in age. We had always talked about when we get old, we won't do this, we won't do that . . . All those conversations were flooding my memory. All our plans never to happen now. I am still sobbing writing this, eight years later.

I was in a black hole for quite a while. Just barely functioning day to day as I imagine everyone feels when they lose a part of themselves. I would sit on my front porch in my rocking chair. Sometimes I would see a little black car coming towards the house and think it was Linda coming to get me. I would pick up the phone to call her as I usually did, daily. It's very different losing a sibling than another family member. It feels like you've lost an arm or a leg and it's difficult to function. After all, you grew up with them. You shared countless memories from birth. You fought. You forgave. You loved. You planned for the future. You planned for spending time together in your old age. There were memories no one could have but the two of you. I was miserable.

I worked and kept tabs on Mom who, of course, was that much older now, and had a little dementia though she would never admit it. She would never talk about Linda and I found that odd. It was like that black cloak fell over her in that regard. I remember feeling a little perturbed that she would talk about Allen's mother and everyone else who had passed, but even though I tried to reach her, she would never talk about Linda. She would change the subject. Mom was good at changing the subject or saying "whatever" if she didn't want to talk about something. I noticed she would have the same clothes on for days at a time. She had a home health aide that came in several times a week and did the basic cleaning and sometimes brought her food. We had ordered meals on wheels for her so we didn't have to worry about her cooking which she didn't care about doing anymore anyway. I would take her to her doctor appointments, and bring her food if I cooked, and pay her bills.

I think it was in November that I needed to get away and Missy had been asking me to come. At that time Linda's friend Diane was also there visiting her sister Martha and we had all made an appointment to see a psychic medium they had seen before. Missy wasn't interested but drove me there. The scheduled meeting was in a large house where the bottom floor was a shop owned by someone else and the medium would come a couple times a month and receive clients upstairs. Martha went first and came down a half hour later, satisfied with her reading. I went next. The first person she brought through was Linda. She described her personality to a tee, talked about her illness, and gave further evidence that her spirit was there. I was in tears when she thanked me for being there for her and taking care of her. The medium then gave me a psychic reading talking about finances, health, and miscellaneous other things. When I came downstairs, the eyes of my friends were on me, waiting . . . When I burst into tears, they knew it was a success. I had been to mediums before, but this was the first time that it really had meaning for me. I never remembered her name and the place shut down, so I never did see her again. I guess that was meant to be as well.

We were all dreading Christmas. Linda had always made such a big deal about it, cooking a fantastic meal, decorating her house, and welcoming friends. We decided we would make it as normal as we could, though every time I went into that house, I could feel the emptiness. And I'm sure Jim didn't want to be there either. Jim decided to cook. Grandmothers were there and we had our usual drinks and appetizers that befitted Christmas. We realized it would never be the same as the woman who made everything special wasn't there to decorate, and cook and just enjoy making everyone happy.

Linda was a hoarder. Every spare room in that house was loaded with stuff to sell on eBay, or gifts in case she needed them, and she loved silver jewelry. She couldn't refuse a bargain, even if she didn't need it. Allen was in a house with all this stuff and would just escape to the den, the room that was his. He left everything as it was. I would go into the bedroom to get something and there was the book Linda was reading with the page turned in to where she was reading and her glasses sitting on the table next to it. It broke my heart.

We had her cremated and we decided at some point in time we would do a memorial service for her. Her friend Jean came a couple of times and paid Allen for truckloads of stuff she would sell on eBay. She and I would become good friends although she eventually told me she never liked me when we first met. Linda had about twenty Yankee candles she had bought on sale. The nursing home was having a benefit for someone, so we hauled off all the Yankee candles and donated them because the people there were so caring and kind to Linda. They were both astonished and grateful. I invited all of Linda's friends to go through her jewelry and take whatever they wanted to keep a piece of her in their hearts. They were hesitant to take anything but when they saw how much there was, they did. Only her closest friends understood that Linda had collected all this because someone might need something, or she would need a gift at a second's notice and so on. She loved people, and only wanted them to be happy and if it was just a little trinket that they loved, or a meal to be made especially for them, she would always follow through. Everyone had a little part of her and there were still tons of jewelry left. Some of it was brand new, never worn. Allen and I decided to have yard sales to get rid of all the items she had collected. We would end up having three yard-sales over the next year or so, putting very low prices on everything, and we got rid of most of what Jean didn't want, or any one of her friends didn't want. Friends helped us and we appreciated their help. I would cringe at the low prices and the value people were getting and I felt if Linda saw this, she would be so angry, but it had to be done for Allen to still function in that house. It was around this time that his mother's health started failing, so he went from taking care of Linda to taking care of his mother. I would cook and bring food to him and Mom, and we would go out to eat once in a while. I knew I had to watch out for both of them. Jim was busy with his job, his life and not right around the corner so that he could not just pop in; besides, I felt he really didn't want to be in that house with his Mom gone.

Jean had emailed me to see if I wanted to go to a day-long workshop Maureen Hancock was having at her house on mediumship and psychic awareness. I didn't know much about who she was, but said sure, I would go. As it turned out, I loved Maureen. She was a comic as well as a medium so she had a great teaching style. Jean and I were both amazed when we were paired up with someone to exchange readings. We both had intuited something for the other person! We thought our imagination was in full force. Maureen did a little gallery reading in the afternoon. She was in front of me giving a reading and turned to me and said, I have a mother here, or mother-in-law. I only knew of one who had passed, my first husband's mother. Maureen said, she's saying "I understand now where you were coming from." That meant a lot to me because I was extremely sorry when I left and made her so angry and hurt with me. That day opened me up to think I could start listening for messages from those who had already passed, and I remembered that incident of waking up and hearing my Grandfather's voice.

It was during the next year that another psychic event was

happening that Jean wanted to go to. Maureen would be there again, and also John Holland, and Karen Paolino Correia. I didn't know any of them but decided to go. I loved John's sense of humor, and of course Maureen; the two of them together were a hoot giving readings and talking about life after death. I was very intrigued with Karen who taught about angels. She had CD's there which I bought and I got her information on courses she taught.

I wanted to take some of Linda's ashes to the Cape that she loved so much. Her friends wanted to be there too. We rented a house for the weekend in a part of the Cape where we'd never stayed before, but it had room enough for all seven of us. We all arrived at different times, and Jean didn't come until the next day. I was so glad Kathy was able to come as we hadn't seen much of her. She had a really hard time, especially after a wine salute, dealing with her loss, and spent most of the first night crying. The next day was the day we would distribute some of the ashes to all of Linda's favorite places. We needed two cars, so it was a caravan going everywhere. We went to the first duplex we stayed at, her favorite fish place, the last condo we stayed at, her favorite Christmas Tree shop. We went to the harbor that she loved with the trees going out into the harbor which took us a while to find again. We all gathered together to toss some ashes in the water and as soon as I tossed them, a wind came and blew them all over Jean and I. We laughed so hard, probably hysterically, because we knew that was Linda's sense of humor. We then went to her favorite gift shop, wandering around until we found it. We crisscrossed all over the place, looking at all the product. I was upstairs and out of the corner of my eye, I saw this lady who reminded me of Linda and she just looked at me and said "This is so much fun, isn't it!" That gave me a chill. Later on, Diane mentioned the lady in the gift shop that reminded her so much of Linda and I told her what she said to me. I was glad we both had the same experience, and I knew it was Linda with us that weekend. When my cousin Cam came to visit that Summer, we took a ride to the cemetery where Dad and Grandad were buried. We bought some flowers to plant and our tools of destruction. We dug a hole next to Dad's stone after cleaning it up and put some ashes in there and with a plant on top. It was very emotional for both of us but we kept the ritual of having a picnic near the gravesite and sharing memories, leaving Dad some jelly beans on his stone. Now Linda was everywhere she wanted to be.

It was in August around Linda's birthday that we had a memorial service. We hired caterers with several tents and tables on the side yard. Everyone came from far and wide. The whole family, friends, some work buddies, our doctor cousins surprised us, and it was lovely. Several of us had written things to say but for some reason, we never did. We were all there in fellowship and love, remembering, and that's just what Linda would have wanted. A celebration of her life. Allen had made a CD with pictures based around a train ride of life. It was beautiful and so appropriate. Anyone who wanted one took one but everyone had viewed it. Allen's Mom had passed in the meantime so he was basically alone and made a routine for himself. He would listen to music, clean the house, mow the lawn and read. He had his own diet he kept to and he was relatively happy at this stage of his life. He and Ron would go to ball games and occasionally concerts.

One day after I came home from work, I kept getting the thought to call Allen as I hadn't called in a couple of days. I did. I asked him if he was eating dinner or something because he sounded weird. He said he hadn't felt good all day. I went over. I took him to the ER because he was showing signs of a stroke. The ER doctor thought maybe it was an illness or something, but I told him, no, he has weakness on his right side. He finally did a CAT scan and found that he had indeed had a stroke. Since he didn't get to a hospital right away, the staff couldn't use stroke buster meds on him. I had called Jim before I took him and he was on the way. Jim stayed with him and in a day or so, they sent him for rehab near Jim. I felt so bad for Allen. Here he had nursed Linda, and then his mother, and when it was time for him to just live his life quietly, he had a stroke. It corrupted some of his speech and some ability on his right side but they thought they could work with it and get him functional again. It was a long process but he was eventually able to come home by himself, though initially he had physical and occupational therapists come to the house. He passed the driving test so he could still drive and he was on meds to prevent it from happening again and saw his doctors regularly. Jim would come and spend weekends with him and organize everything for him. He was going to make sure to take care of his Dad.

I was buying groceries for Mom and checking on her daily. Her memory had failed. I gave up on making sure she bathed or changed her clothes and just picked my battles with her. I remember thinking, thank God it's me looking after her and not Linda. Linda had no tolerance for what she thought should be, and wouldn't be happy with the way things were going. As long as she was eating some and taking her meds, that's all that mattered.

I had had enough of winter so started spending a month in Florida near Barbara. It was like going home for me. I loved the weather and I loved Florida. I would always tell Mom and her doctors that I was leaving and her health care aide would give her more time. Mom always said, stick your feet in the sand for me and have a good time.

10

A Tiny Spark of Light

I was still working about 16 hours a week. I decided to do a course online with Karen Paolino Correia on certified angel oracle card reading. It was perfect because it was online, something new to me. I was very interested in angels and found that I could use the cards to give readings. The course pushed me to explore myself and push myself out of my fog. I met some lovely ladies with whom I still keep in touch, four years later. Towards the end of the course, she took one night to talk about mediumship. We were to give a reading to someone in our group, but while Karen was talking about it and doing a meditation, I was talking in my head to a man. He was giving me information about his life, what he looked like, what he was wearing and I knew he was related to Karen. I thought, well this is bizarre. I wonder if this is actually real. After the class, I emailed Karen and gave her all the information. Well, I never heard back from her so figured I was crackers. The next class we had, she said offhandedly to me, Oh, I'm sorry it took so long to respond to you, but that's my uncle so and so who comes through a lot and all the information was spot on. I was stunned. That little intuitive voice in me was awakened and I thank Karen to this day for pushing us. I started thinking differently, that maybe I could occasionally talk to those who had passed. But I felt unworthy and questioned how someone like me could be able to do that. My life hasn't been one of religion, church, or charity. I did though, find my first spiritual tribe, and we bought oracle cards and read for each other. I also gained a lot of information on the angelic world. Most of the readings were psychic, but it gave me a network to see what was going on in that world. My spirit tribe was in motion.

People were talking about going to Omega institute in Rhinebeck, New York to attend classes. I googled Omega and got a list of all their courses. I saw that John Holland and Lauren Rainbow were doing a course on mediumship. I yearned to do it, but refused to sign up for something I knew I wasn't prepared for, and neither was I going to go someplace I'd never been, and spend time with people I didn't know. I was always an introvert and don't warm up to anyone until I've known them for a while. I ditched that idea. But then it popped up again, when someone mentioned it. The course was for all levels, beginner to advanced. I got up the nerve and signed up. In my head, I heard my guides and those in spirit cheering! I wasn't so happy. They didn't have any single rooms left so I had to bunk in a cabin with a stranger. Okay, I was officially off my rocker. Going to New York, taking a course I didn't think I belonged in, and staying with a complete stranger. The truth is I was scared shitless. On my two-hour trek, I beseeched my guides and helpers to stay with me and protect me so that I wouldn't make a fool out of myself. I could feel their laughter.

I checked in with no sign of the roommate. I met a couple of other women on the other side of our cabin, had a vegetarian dinner and went to the welcome meeting. It wasn't until later that night that my roomie Joan showed up. She was sweet and quiet and just as nervous as I was. She was taking the same course. We all were. She was not far from Illinois, so had come further than I for this week. Overall, it was a great week. I loved John and Lauren. We did many exercises and learned a lot about the spirit world and ourselves. We met a bunch of like-minded people, some who would become friends for a long time. I did learn that I could indeed talk to spirits. We practiced many exercises. I especially liked it when one of us was blindfolded, we played musical chairs, and you had to read for whomever sat in front of you. I seemed to be able to hone-in much better to the spirit world when I was blindfolded! I took to shutting my eyes when I was doing a reading, which would come back to bite me in the ass later on as Mavis wouldn't let you close your eyes; *your eyes are the mirror to your soul.* But I get ahead of myself again. The whole week was awe- inspiring and most of us wondered what we would do to continue this in the future. Luckily, they started a Facebook group with all the participants and some of us decided to practice every week online using skype. We learned a lot and there were quite a few in the group. It was different reading on-line but we found that it didn't matter.

We learned that John Holland was doing an advanced mediumship group with Janet Nohavec for a weekend in Maine. A few of us from our Wednesday group decided to go, though we didn't know if we were advanced or not. We did want to see Janet as we had heard a lot about her. Ultimately, we didn't need to worry about how advanced we were; we were no more or less advanced than anyone else there. We did learn a few new exercises to do and it was a joy to watch Janet give readings. She was amazing. We already knew John was!

When the moderator for our mediumship development group decided she didn't want to lead it anymore, we decided to do our own group. There were about 10 of us who were dedicated to meeting every week, so we continued. Eventually Kim, a fellow medium, got a free zoom account which meant we could only be on for 45 minutes before we got charged, so eventually Kim bought a professional account. Along with our group, I started practicing on all my friends. I would use skype, but eventually got my own zoom account. Some readings were good, some not so good, but they put up with me and supported me. Since Linda passed, Diane's sister Martha passed and so did Linda's friend Kathy, both with pancreatic cancer. I tried reading for Diane but Martha came in with such loving energy for her sister, that I couldn't control the emotion and cried. I would need to learn to control the feelings spirit gave me. I remember Colin Bates, an English medium, telling us to just let it flow through, and out. I did some amazing readings. I read for Jean, and her sister came through talking about childhood memories and a fractured leg or arm. Jean was stunned. She had known about her sister's arm but no-one knew the circumstances except she and her sister. Sometimes I would wonder where that information came from as it just dropped into my head. Sometimes spirit would come in and no-one would recognize who they were. This would confound us sometimes as we knew that those who passed, don't show up unless there is someone in the room they are connected to, or who can pass on a message. It would take me awhile to just blurt out what I heard, saw or knew. I was always afraid it was just my imagination. After all, Dad always said I had a vivid imagination. (Now I thank him for reminding me of that.) We were now in the loop, and had contact with many mediums and teachers on the Facebook page, so we could pick and choose who we wanted to study with next. I still remembered my trance days and my table tipping days. I saw that Tony Stockwell was doing a trance week at Omega in the Summer and decided I wanted to do it. Kim said she'd go too, so we both signed up and rented a room off campus together since it was cheaper, although we still had to pay for the food. Omega had a new chef and people said the food was better.

The week of the class, I drove to the airport to pick Kim up. We went right to Omega because we wanted to check in early and get comfortable. This time we skipped the welcome night class and went straight to the hotel. Class began the next day. We got there when the dining room opened up, had breakfast and then headed to class, not knowing what to expect or what Tony would be like. Well, as most people do, you fall in love with Tony as he is funny and down to earth with everyone. We started that day going into trance. It was an amazing week. We met more wonderful people and did some great trance work along with mediumship and healing work. We had confirmation of who some of our guides were, as several people saw my guide, Blue Eagle, and Kim had a past life regression session, where her guide showed up. We were exhausted every day and hit the gift shop quite a few times too, buying books and trinkets. We hit it off with an English lady named Edith who did healing on us, and we did some on her and she eventually joined our Wednesday group but only for a short time as she was always traveling. One night, Tony said he would do a trance demonstration for the class. We arrived and the room was shrouded and dark with red lights stationed all around. Someone asked if they could take pictures, and it was permitted as long as there was no noise or flash. Later on, pictures were posted to our group and you could clearly see spirit. George directed the sitting and picked those in the audience who would come up for readings. I never saw anything like it in my life and the energy in that room was other-worldly. You could actually see the spirit people coming into Tony's aura and one by one the people stood in front of him receiving their message, with most of them sobbing when they came back, just for the high energy they felt from him and sometimes the message itself from their own loved one. A spirit came through Tony that said they had never walked on Earth. I questioned Tony about it at the end and he told me it was "Star" his angel, who rarely comes through Tony when he is in trance. Immediately after I asked the question, Tony asked if anyone knew a Jason. No-one raised their hand except me. My cousin Dave changed his name to Jason. Tony said he came in on my vibration since I asked a question. I knew he was trying to communicate something since he passed very recently. He kept making his presence known and I knew there was unfinished business between his sister Cam and himself and I had to find a way to make that happen. Trance with Tony is something you need to see once in your lifetime if you're interested in it. We got more telephone numbers from people and headed home with our head in the clouds. It would take a couple of days to come down from that experience. Kim and I got along well and had no issues sleeping in the same room! I would end up moving close to her in Florida. I loved her energy. She is like a daughter/friend to me and a kind and generous person. I had stayed in touch with Sally who had been doing trance for a while and we started practicing trance on skype once a week and then it went to twice a week. We heard from a lot of guides. It was fun, and inspiring. I intuitively knew I would go further with mediumship, and she will be taking trance onward and eventually teaching it, so our practices stopped although we still remain friends.

With that class, there was a whole new group of people we could interact with on the internet as the groups were always posted on Facebook. We heard that Tony was having an online mentorship program on many different topics so Kim and I signed up. It was a year-long event. There was a financial cost, but the gain was more and more knowledge. Never did we think we were doing all of this in order to be paid. It would be nice, but making money was not our motivation. Tony had his own following of people that seemed to show up for everything he did. He was amazingly interesting. He is a free spirit and sometimes changed what he was going to talk about in mid-stream and you knew information was being downloaded from spirit. He made us think about a lot of different aspects of mediumship, and the occult world. We talked about trance, about physical mediumship which we actually did when we were young by making the table dance around, extra-terrestrials, reincarnation and just about anything one could imagine. We were glad we took the mentorship and were amazed at his thought processes and how much he knew.

It was October and I kept getting the nudge to go to the Cape as spirit had a surprise for me. But I didn't want to go. That was Linda's place, not mine. After several more nudges from the spirit world, I gave in and booked a hotel room. I had no idea why I was going, but knew I was going by myself. The room was in a cheap crappy hotel but I figured I only needed to sleep in it. I could walk to the beach, although it was a long walk. I took a tour of all the places we used to go, and even included a fish dinner. Nothing surprised me. I went to the harbor where Linda's ashes had blown in our faces and I felt a little blue. As I was leaving, I looked up and out to my right. There was a huge stone angel overlooking the harbor where we put her ashes.

I stopped dead! They had been building a funky church when we were last there but the angel wasn't there. Apparently, that was what all the nudging was about. They were telling me angels watched over Linda and it was a good spot for her ashes. Well, after that, I just left in the middle of the night. Why should I stay? I had my surprise.

I hated to leave my little girl Georgia as she was ill. She had cancer in her nasal passage and we tried everything to alleviate her discomfort. She had gone to her other Mom for the weekend. I had started to give her pain meds as she had a hard time now going up and down stairs and would continually sneeze blood and mucus. I had never heard of it but the vet said it actually was common in dogs with a pointed snout. Cats too. She was my sweetie pie and I hated to see her deteriorate but I was determined I wouldn't let her suffer like Chinook obviously did, because I couldn't let go. When she was basically crawling up the steps, I said, it's time. I made an appointment with her vet and drove her there, stopping at McDonald's to get her a hamburger on the way. The vet examined her and said, yes, you're right. I sat on the floor holding her and crying. Another beautiful soul gone. I called her other Mom on the way home. I realize I should have given her a chance to say goodbye too, but she had just been with them. They were heartbroken too. I know some people refuse to get another pet after losing a lovely animal, but I believe your love is not to be kept to yourself but given away and who better than an animal that needs that love.

My sister from another mother, Jean, told me that John Holland was coming to her town and going to be at a small venue and I should come with her. It was cold, so it must have been around November. I went and stayed overnight at Jean's and we attended the small event. We never expected a reading at any of these events, we just liked to go and see how the mediums worked. We were sitting and chatting before the start and in a lull, all of a sudden, this *whoosh* of cold air came barreling down the center aisle. Jean looked at me and I looked at her and we both said, "Did you feel that?" at the same time. It was crazy. Everyone around us was just talking with each other. Well, later on, we discovered what that *whoosh* was about. John gave a reading to someone and as he was finishing, he drank some water and was doodling on a pad. He said, "This will sound crazy but did someone bury some ashes under a Christmas tree?" and he had drawn a tree. Jean poked me in the ribs and said, It's Linda, raise your hand, it's the Christmas Tree Shop!" I raised my hand and told John and the others it was at a Christmas Tree Shop. He laughed. He went on to say there was a group of friends together and on and on. I told him yes, there were two cars of friends driving around the cape distributing ashes. Now we knew what the cold air was—Linda was telling us she was coming! As much as we knew about life after death, it's wonderful when you get spectacular evidence like that. We talked about it all night. Every medium wants the wow factor but it's really not necessary. Sometimes it's just an *I Love You* from a lost spouse or other relationship.

It was around this time I decided to bite the bullet and move to Florida. Mom refused to go with me, which I couldn't understand because she was from the south herself. I guess when you're 96, you've had enough of everything and just want to be left alone. She had help in place and Allen would go see her and so would Jim and Hannah. She had fallen a few times but luckily hadn't hurt herself but I noticed a little confusion afterwards that only lasted a little while. I told her aide, if she falls again, she cannot refuse to go to the hospital. She may have been having mini strokes. But all in all, she was functioning at home with help. I had looked over the winter for a place, but didn't find a condo I wanted, so I was still looking. I put my house on the market and had yard sales to get rid of all the stuff I didn't want to move with me. There was quite a bit. I had a rule that once it left the house, it didn't come back in, so everything that didn't sell went to the Salvation Army. There were several car loads. I asked Jim and Hannah if they wanted my furniture as I wasn't about to move it all. They were grateful and took most of it. It was a good little house for me but I felt it was time to move on and I hoped the new owners would enjoy it as much as I did. I found a condo online which was kind of funny. I asked my realtor to go look at it but she couldn't find it on realtor.com. When I went to look again, it was gone. I knew I wanted it sight unseen. The next day she texted me and said it came online again. She went to look at it and called me while doing so and we made an offer that was accepted. Jim and Hannah got a truck and moved my stuff over to Allen's garage and took the rest to their house. Dan the plumber helped with his pickup truck. So, there I was in limbo at Allen's until I closed on the condo and could get down to Florida. Cousin Cam came to visit one last time while I was there. I had told her about her brother Dave/Jason popping in at the end of Tony's trance class, and he also popped in while I was being healed. I knew there were things left unsaid between Cam and he, so I set up a little trance session between Cam and me, hoping her brother would come in. He did! Cam said she heard him talking to her before I even spoke. He told her all the things he wanted to say to her and she got to voice what she wanted to say. It was a healing for both of them and Cam was so grateful. We took another picnic trip to the gravesite and this time put some of her brother's ashes in with her Dad's. Of course, we brought jelly beans again for Dad. We would never go back there. I wouldn't. Cam might, because her Mom will be interred with her Dad.

I again offered to take Mom with me to Florida, even for a couple of weeks but she refused. She said "I'll be here when you get back." I knew intuitively she wouldn't, but just smiled and said okay and that I loved her. I was always worried when I left her but through the years, I decided it was time for me to live my life. I begged her to come with me but she always refused. When you're that age, you don't want change of any kind. I gave up. I made sure her aide put in more hours and talked to Allen and Jim to make sure she was well taken care of. That was no problem with any of them. I also told her doctor and they already had my phone number and Jim's.

There was a snafu with the movers and they arrived before I got there, but my realtor was there to let them in and they dumped everything in the living room. I arrived in September right after a hurricane so I didn't know if anything was still standing but luckily, we didn't get the effects of it at all.

I loved the condo. It was right on a pond and all the birds came the first week I was there to welcome me. The sand cranes would walk right by my porch and look in and honk all the while. I was in heaven. I would sit out there for hours. It took a while to settle in and unpack all those boxes, buy some furniture and make the place my own. I made a few friends and joined the volunteer ambulance department, becoming an ambulance driver. Of course, I had to take a course and go through training but it was a fabulous free service for everyone living there. I never let anyone know I was a medium as they were all rigid church going people and I didn't want to scare them or skew their opinion of me. Eventually, I didn't care, and I did let friends know the work I did on the side. I was still doing trance online with Sally and doing readings on line. I had my own website and filed the papers for my LLC. It was not like I was getting bookings right and left but I was prepared. I did have four or five people that signed up and I gave readings via zoom. I always knew that spirit would show up although I was always worried about being there for them, and interpreting things correctly. In a little way, I still wondered where this gift was coming from and why it came to me.

In October, Mom's aide called and said Mom fell again. Should she make her go to the hospital. I told her definitely yes. Mom was mad but she had no choice this time for her own good. She hadn't broken anything although she complained of pain all over. We decided to send her to the nursing home for rehab. They started rehab but she always complained that it hurt too much. Her doctor had another x-ray taken but they didn't find anything. We decided to give up her apartment and have her stay in the nursing home. We took some of her things over to her and she basically went downhill from there. When I called her, she practically didn't know who I was. She thought I was still on vacation and didn't remember I moved. On Christmas eve the nursing home called me and said she was in such pain, they thought they would take her to the hospital. They told me she hadn't fallen or anything and in fact could not get out of bed by herself. Knowing Mom, I thought she might try if they hadn't gotten to her room in a prompt manner! They took another x-ray at the hospital and didn't find anything. The next day was Christmas and the ER doctor called me and said she was in so much pain that they did a total body scan and found a hip fracture that really couldn't be repaired at her age. I was furious. I felt that something happened at the nursing home that someone was covering up and filed a complaint with the manager and she talked to everyone who said she hadn't fallen. There was nothing I could do.

Jim and Hannah had come to Allen's for Christmas and Jim went to the hospital and said he would stay at Allen's and just be with her. They were keeping her medicated for pain and I'm sure she was out of it. I knew exactly what would occur. I felt it in my heart and I knew she would pass on the 27th. That morning, they called Jim and he stayed with her and held her hand and I asked him to play certain music. He loved his grandmother and it was really hard for him. They all said, there was no reason for me to be there, but I was there in spirit and was spiritually waiting, and later on, Mom would come speak through a prominent medium and say she knew I was there holding her hand. I argued that no, I wasn't there, it was Jim, but she said yes, he was there, but she could also feel my presence. Jim called in tears and I knew she was gone. Another death he had to mourn. Even though I tried to prepare her, Mom was afraid of dying. I knew who was there waiting for her, Linda, Dad, Grandad, her brother and sister. But it took her a day to realize it all and I felt a sense of lightness when she did. Also, I came out of the bathroom and my smoke alarm started going off. It had never gone off, and never did again. You see Linda was great at modifying electrical or technical equipment. She would screw up our phones when I went to meet Jean, she would flash lights on and off, turn off car equipment, etc. You get the picture. I would later find out that Mom didn't do it, she said Linda did, "she likes all that stuff."

I heard from Jim and he told me Allen took a fall outside and shattered his knee cap. Luckily someone was right there and called an ambulance. He would go into surgery to repair it but wouldn't be able to straighten it or walk on that leg afterwards. That was his good leg, not the one that was weak from the stroke! Jim went about putting a bed downstairs for him and getting a ramp so he could get into the house. I was going to drive up in June.

In January, I adopted a little Pekinese dog. She is sweetie pie number two. She and her brother had been given to a rescue. I'm sure she was used as a breeding dog and when she couldn't perform any longer, they turned her in. She was afraid of people. I'm sure she was just kept in a kennel all the time. She was being fostered in a house with seven other dogs so seemed to socialize well with other dogs. She took to the princess life very fast and very well. We walked every day and she was as good as gold. She never barked unless some other dog barked, and she was very clean. When Jim and Hannah came for a visit, they spent time with her and I owe them, as they worked with her so she would socialize with people. They knew how to treat scared dogs and she now likes people.

The more I thought about it, the more I hated to think about driving. In the meantime, my plumber friend Dan texted me and said he wanted a reading. Something happened to him that he couldn't resolve. He also said he and his wife had been separated for over a year. Uh oh . . .I told him I'd see him in June when I came up. I decided to fly up there with Honey. It was a very expensive trip as I had to basically buy a seat for her. I knew I could use Allen's car once I was there. Ron picked me up at the airport and brought me to Allen's and we had pizza and chatted a while. It was really hard seeing Linda's house in such disarray with mail and other clutter all over the place. It had a new vibe that immediately put me on edge. Not the loving, welcoming home I was used to. There was a bed in the dining room and everything looking like two bachelors lived there. Allen still had Daisy and someone up the street had taken her in while Allen was in hospital but she was back with Allen now. They volunteered to still walk her but since I was there, I would walk both dogs. That got old really soon as Daisy was not a good walker. She was also overweight from too many cookies. She lost a little weight while Allen was in hospital but she had a long way to go. She was small but a sturdy girl but she felt like a bag of cement if you picked her up! Allen had nurses and physical and occupational therapists coming in as he had just arrived a day before I did. He used a walker and it was very hard for him. I tried to pick up and organize things and cook and then Jim and Hannah came often to take care of things. I made a date to meet with Dan one night.

He told me to just go in the house, and told me where the key was because something came up. I was used to going in his house and sometimes taking his dog for a walk so I was glad to see her. He wanted me to try and connect with a spirit, but the energy was not favorable so we just talked. I was in an energy funk being in Linda's house and seeing Allen so bad off, knowing that everything in that town was ending for me. Jim had found a place for Allen to live close to him and Hannah, and he would be moving him at the end of June. Hannah decided she would take Daisy home on a weekend to see if she got along with their two big dogs. Jim had his doubts but it actually worked. They all found their own space. Daisy never came back home and they moved Allen. When they were ready to leave, I just cried. I was so strung out with emotions by then, I didn't know what to do. Jim gave me a hug and the next day he would take me to the airport to go home. Dan and I texted on and off but that's where we left it.

11

Into the Light

We had been following the British mediums and there was a spiritualist college in England that was on our bucket list. We never thought we would be experienced enough to go. I especially wanted to see Mavis Pitilla. She had been a renowned medium for 50 years and when we found she would be holding a class in Florida, Kim and I signed up. I heard that Mavis can look at you and read your soul. She could see your colors and determine if you are a medium or not. She knew if there was a spirit with you—she knew it all. We were determined to get up in front of Mavis and give a reading. Kim had already been doing an online mentorship with her and loved her. Mavis knew all there was to know about mediumship, the afterlife, everything you would want to know. She always said, it's just her opinion, but I would find that her opinion resonated with my soul more than any other teacher I had studied with.

Suzanne Giesemann was promoting and putting on the week long class. I had read Suzanne's books and was moved. She had studied under Mavis and was a great medium in her own right and did a lot of work with parents who had lost children. I admired her. She also wrote Mavis's biography. There was a platform mediumship class the following weekend but we didn't feel we were ready for that!

We rented a room and took off for the Villages. It was exciting to see Mavis in person. I was scared shitless. What if she looked in my soul and told me I wasn't a medium?

It was a great class. The first day though, Mavis wasn't feeling too well. by the next day, she had to leave halfway through the day and we were told she was hospitalized that night with pneumonia. Her partner Jean carried on with Suzanne. It was in one of these circles where mediums were doing readings that fisherman Bill first appeared. The woman brought in a man dressed in yellow rain suit fishing garb, he had a fishing boat and it was up North. She went on to describe him and I raised my hand. Only thing wrong was I thought he was still alive! That was a long time ago but her description and evidence led me to believe it was him. I started trying to find information about his death and engaged friends who had more internet options, but none of us could find anything, so I gave up looking. To this day, I like to give evidence in readings that the client has to follow up on because it's so much more evidential.

Kim and I thought we would not get a chance to make fools of ourselves in front of Mavis. We were fine with it, all we wanted was for Mavis to get better. She came back Thursday night and taught the class on Friday. We each did have the experience of getting up in a group with Mavis sitting right next to me. I got up, I had a contact, but was so nervous I lost it. She told me to sit down. I knew my worst fears were realized. Then she said something like "I'm sure you don't want the gift of mediumship in your family to end with you, after all you are third generation medium on your mother's side." I almost passed out and had to hold back my tears. I thought she was saying I wouldn't make it. But what she really meant was, I was third generation medium. It was time to buckle down and get it right. Kim had the opportunity to get up also and she did fine, though she thought she didn't. She never thinks she does well, but she always does. That is her lesson to learn, kind of like mine. I found that Mavis was doing another mentorship that started in January and I was able to sign up for that. I wanted to learn everything I could from this lady. She explained the spirit world and the most important part of being a medium, is knowing yourself first. So that is what I concentrated on. Knowing myself. It has been a long haul but she gave us the tools to do it. I had been meditating for quite a while now (something I swore I'd never do) but Mavis called it a discipline. We learned quite a few disciplines, including how to contact those guardians and inspirers in spirit who are working with us. We had picked the right teacher. She still scared me and I rarely raised my hand when she wanted someone to read in our group. The biggest thing she told me was to just relax and let it go and let it flow. I remember that every time I give a reading. Being a medium is not an easy calling. Especially in the beginning. You are always sure it's your imagination making things up, so you don't want to give the information you are receiving from the spirit world, because you may be wrong. I had to forget all the experiences and challenges of my youth that formed the person I was. You can't just say, "I'm a medium" and go out in the public without knowing the repercussions of what you say and do. You need empathy for the public and the spirit world and above all else, respect those in spirit, and do no harm. Spirit are people, and also need the healing you can provide them by getting their message to their loved one.

The other thing Mavis told us, was that every person on this earth contains a spark of the creator. It usually takes an illness or traumatic event in a medium's life for the light to turn on and your soul to awaken to your path. *I knew then that Linda's passing was my spark event.* I really believe that this was all a plan we had arranged before we were born. Her passing from the earth plane would trigger my mediumship. Now, I thank her for her gift. There have been times I've sat and said to them, why am I still here, I want to be with you. What I would hear in return was, "You have work to do." I will discuss my thoughts on "light," further on down the line.

Our mentorship with Tony ended and our mentorship with

Mavis was ending in a few months but we already knew we would be continuing with Mavis. The next time she offered a platform mediumship weekend, we signed up. What could we lose? We could only gain. It was an amazing weekend. A lot of mediums were stepping out of their comfort zone and a lot were beginning to do demonstrations as a business. When I got up, I bombed again. I had to find a way to stop my nerves from destroying me. I had good evidence for Mavis's partner Jean, and she recognized what I was trying to say. I regretted that I let Jean's relative down. On the last day, I got up again and did not mess up. I saw a man, I knew he was an uncle, he liked baseball and he gave me the name of his favorite team. I knew he would take road-trips going to different baseball parks. Kim could accept everything. I received solid evidence and stayed with the flow. Afterwards, I felt much better. It was actually fun. Mavis expects more of us now that we've been with her for over a year, and rightfully so. Now I raise my hand first because I know, this is the reason I'm in this class, to learn and grow and practice. There is no more comfort zone.

Four of us from our Wednesday group decided to go for it and signed up for a class at Arthur Findlay College in England. AFC as everyone calls it, has been around for centuries and is the *World's foremost college for the advancement of spiritualism and psychic sciences.* There are many classes held there and with many subjects including mediumship, trance work, automatic writing, physical mediumship and so forth. We looked at the program and signed up for Chris Drew's Story telling week with Chris, Lynn Probert and several other tutors. We let Jean and Mavis know we were going, and they were friends with Chris, so Jean gave him our names to be sure we were put with either Chris or Lynn. We started a year in advance to plan it, and were on line with each other continually about hotels, restaurants, sight-seeing and even what we were packing because we decided to sight-see while we were there. We would go to Arthur Findley College after two nights in London, from there, pick up a car (Holy cow driving on the wrong side!) and go to Stonehenge, Bath, Glastonbury, the Cotswolds and then to Edinburgh. We would be gone two and a half weeks.

The time finally arrived and Kim and I flew out of Orlando overnight and then hit the ground running. We took all kinds of holistic medicine so as not to get sick and not have jet lag. And we didn't. We saw the sights in London and took a limo drive to AFC. We checked in and were interviewed by Chris whom we immediately loved. He had a list at his interview table with our names on it! I ended up in the class with Lynn and loved her. We soon understood that we should not have been afraid to go. We were mediums, just like everyone else. Some kept coming back to these classes, for twenty years or more. We knew that wouldn't be us, but we would go back. I got sick and ended up having to walk down the hill to the surgery and see Doc Martin, (ha ha). Several in my class were sick but they bounced back. When I get sick, I get pneumonia or bronchitis and need antibiotics to recuperate. I recently had a journey with my guide, Blue Eagle, and he told me that my lung issues were from my past life as a Lakota Sioux woman. Some folks don't believe in past lives, but I do. I've had many instances of evidence to the contrary, especially about that Lakota life.

I did get to see the lovely little town of Stansted since I was walking all around looking for the pharmacy! For the rest of the week, I would sit near the door in class so I could escape when I started coughing so as not to disturb anyone. I did have the opportunity to stand up in the class and demonstrate and got very good evidence. I was probably too tired to be nervous! I saw an English gentleman who would walk down to the local pub every night. I felt his personality and knew he was a cantankerous sort. He was recognized immediately. I knew he was a neighbor. He kept directing me to his shoes which were really big galoshes that were all dirty and muddy. I also saw him giving vegetables to his neighbors. He indeed was a neighbor to one of the mediums there and his personality was right on point.

His galoshes were pertinent because he had a chicken coop in back of the apartment building and was always wet and dirty. He wanted to say hello and thank the medium for being kind to such a cantankerous person that he was. We met so many nice people and Chris did a spiritual assessment on me which was amazing. Among other things, he told me my mediumship was right on the edge of being powerful and just amazing. He also told me I would be moving again because he saw me writing a published book but he saw me writing it on the beach. I told him I just moved and I'm 20 minutes from the beach. He said, "No, you're moving again." Having just moved two months ago, I thought he was crazy, but my Uncle George had come through a medium friend and said the same thing about a year ago. Interesting.

Just to be in Stansted Hall with so much history, was an experience for a lifetime, and I would urge anyone to give it a go at least once because it's worth the trip. The rest of our trip was amazing. We were told by locals that Stonehenge was nice to see but we probably wouldn't feel the energy there. They were so wrong. As we were driving and saw it in the distance, we felt a chill. Every one of us. When we did arrive and started walking around the stones, I felt one of my guides stand behind me and my medium friends also felt their guides. This was a sacred place for them. Some of us could spiritually see the workers who had been there to erect the stones. It was crowded with people and the stones were roped off but it didn't matter. We could still be in our own space and feel the energy. This was not my main guide, Blue Eagle. This was a guide I only caught a glimpse of once or twice and when Chris Drew did a spiritual reading on me, he saw him also and was taken aback by his energy and his eyes. He is clearly someone in my tribe who has all the answers. I will keep working on establishing a closer relationship with him.

From there we drove to Bath where we had an appointment for high tea the next day as well as seeing the Roman Baths. Well, we got into a little trouble driving to our hotel. We were directed down this dirt road and when we realized our mistake, we couldn't turn around. I was driving and as I was trying to turn, we hit the gutter and realized that a tire had blown. Off to our right was a dead-end street so we drove the car there, hoping to get to a phone. As we were pulling into someone's driveway, a lovely lady came running out saying our tire was flat and we weren't going anywhere; come in the back and have a drink while we sort it out. They had been celebrating a neighbor's anniversary, so were pretty sloshed, but her husband volunteered to change the tire. When we looked, there was no spare! These lovely people called a cab and a tow truck and said they would wait up for the tow truck to come. We were totally flustered about the flat tire, but we all realized, if we hadn't gotten the flat tire we would never have met these kind and generous English folk. Spirit at work. Eventually the car got sorted out after we had to take a taxi to our high tea. Bath was historically interesting to me. The high tea was wonderful and we loved Bath. From there we drove to Glastonbury and from there to Edinburgh where we toured all the places that inspired JK Rowling and her Harry Potter books. I will one day go back to Scotland and tour more of the countryside. We made memories and were sad to go home!

Fisherman Bill would keep coming back to our Wednesday group and other practices and usually he would talk about himself, as that's how he was on earth, completely narcissistic, but the last, (and I hope final) time he came through Kim, he showed his true personality here on earth and how ugly he was to me. At the end of his visit though, Kim said, "his soul is crying for forgiveness". I held no anger or animosity towards him. I forgave him a long time ago. It always takes two, and I allowed the bad behavior. That was my lesson. I believe when we pass from this earth, we have a life review, and I'm sure that's what Bill was going through, as I've seen it again and again with some of the readings I've done. Another time, Mom came through a medium friend to speak to me. She had communicated many times before, but this time she said that she never showed sorrow over Linda's passing because if she did, she would never go back to sanity. She shut down her feelings many years ago during a heartbreaking time. I know it was when her brother passed. So that answered my question about why she wouldn't talk about Linda. Our loved ones always have a reason to communicate with us from the other side. She knew I was always puzzled about that.

I would soon find out also that not only dead people communicate with us. I was giving a reading in our practice group, saw this gentleman clearly, knew he was a grandfather and saw him strolling and talking to his grandson. He showed me his profession and also showed me working on a car and teaching his grandson about cars. At the end, the medium I was giving the reading to said her father was still alive! He was, but he had dementia so bad that he didn't recognize her any longer. He clearly communicated to her that he was fine and living mostly in the spirit world. This happens with dementia patients and also with those in comas. The accuracy of it was amazing to me. She said he was afraid to die, when last they communicated. He is not afraid any longer.

There is no hell, or punishment when you pass. Only loving guidance for everyone, no matter what you did on this earth. Bill was allowed to come through, mainly for me to be aware he was gone but it took a few times for him to ask forgiveness. After the last visit, I inadvertently found a death notice but no obituary. He had passed just before that first visit of his. No one knows how, but one of the mediums did see him falling out of his boat. I'm sure that's the way he would have wanted to pass.

Mavis taught us how to go into the silence and make a space to visit with our guides. In this way, you can talk to your guides and ask them what you can do to be a better medium on your end, and you can also ask them to bring things to you in a specific way so you "get it" more clearly. Mediumship is all about energy. It's not like a loved one is standing in front of you in solid form, passing on information.

We have to interpret pictures we get, vocal messages, smells, seeing images, and just having words drop into our consciousness. But I digress, I took a little journey one day to sit with my guides and to get to know all of them. When I walked into the room where I meet them, I saw a blond woman in white whom I've never seen before. I asked her who she was and she said "Charmaine". My gypsy. Not like any gypsy I imagined! I was awe struck because I thought I imagined that name as a child.

This book has been in my mind for many years but I didn't want it to be like every book ever written so I put the book writing idea down every time it came to me. There is something to be said for timing. It was part of Chris's spiritual reading and I finally listened. I needed to be safe and comfortable with myself. I needed to have Mavis's spiritual strength that she taught me, and Jean's instruction on speaking my word. I needed to have my physical and spiritual tribe to urge me on.

When I talk about "into the light", I don't mean it figuratively. I mean into the light, which each and every one of us was given when we were born. Given to us by the great Spirit, God, Jesus, whatever you are comfortable with calling this great presence of love. I have had to travel within to ignite my light, and with Linda's help, I did. Many intuitives, psychics, or mediums are not aware of their gifts until something happens that alters their way of thinking, whether it be an illness, a traumatic event, or the death of a loved one. I know many who don't think they've ignited their light, but there they are, doing good deeds, loving Mother Earth, loving the animal kingdom, showing kindness when it's not expected, doing the very best they can in this world. I could go on and on. We all have that light. I am no different than anyone else except for the choices I made in the last eight years. It has taken me a lifetime to develop my spiritual gift and I pray I have time to do good and give healing to both the spirit world and those on earth.

Just last night, we had a practice session with six mediums. I received an email from one of them this morning about the reading I did. To me, it was rather ordinary and not a fantastic reading. This is the email: Titled "Holy Smokes". *I just had to let you know that I spoke with John's brother tonight after our session and he was able to validate much of what you shared tonight! He was thrilled and so thankful. I'll share next week the details but you gotta love how spirit works. Great job. John and his brother are so very thankful to you and the cool thing is that his angelversary is just six days away. You gave a wonderful gift to this family tonight and right before the angelversary.* (Names have been changed to protect privacy.)

I'm not including that to be boastful or anything because it was quite ordinary to me, but it was not ordinary to that man in spirit who wanted so badly to come through and talk to this brother and let him know he was still alive and grateful. This is the true meaning of mediumship, to heal both worlds. Just because they are in spirit doesn't mean they've gone to a place they can't be reached. Spirit is so intelligent. They probably had this planned for weeks, as the medium who wrote me doesn't come every week. The loved ones in spirit are wheelers and dealers and manage to set up a communication when they want. It always amazes me. If it stops being amazing, we should hang up our hat, because it is a truly amazing gift and one that shouldn't be taken lightly. This gift involves work. Learning never stops for us. Just like my sister Linda, whenever I'm practicing with someone new who is a little nervous, she is the one who comes through and gives great evidence for the medium to present. She loves to help, so we are both working for the great spirit, she from across the veil and me, from right here.

Where I go from here, I'm not sure, and I'm not worried. I do know I will continue to study with Mavis and Jean as long as I can. I will keep pushing myself out of my comfort zone because that's how we grow. I will always be grateful for the nearby ocean that fills my heart with the energy I need to continue this journey. Yes, I did move. I am now almost right on the ocean so I can walk there every morning and night. Thank you, Chris. I also took a course in basic shamanism which was great and I have more learning to do there. Kim and I realized we were shamans, and I have no doubt we were together in the Lakota world in a past life. You're never too young or old to develop this gift. You just have to trust in yourself above all, and know that you are worthy and loved.

Printed in the United States
By Bookmasters